T0326593

# International Perspectives on Artificial Intelligence

# International Perspectives on
# Artificial Intelligence

Edited by
J. Mark Munoz and Alka Maurya

ANTHEM PRESS

Anthem Press
An imprint of Wimbledon Publishing Company
*www.anthempress.com*

This edition first published in UK and USA 2022
by ANTHEM PRESS
75–76 Blackfriars Road, London SE1 8HA, UK
or PO Box 9779, London SW19 7ZG, UK
and
244 Madison Ave #116, New York, NY 10016, USA

© 2022 J. Mark Munoz and Alka Maurya editorial matter and selection;
individual chapters © individual contributors

The moral right of the authors has been asserted.

All rights reserved. Without limiting the rights under copyright reserved above,
no part of this publication may be reproduced, stored or introduced into
a retrieval system, or transmitted, in any form or by any means
(electronic, mechanical, photocopying, recording or otherwise),
without the prior written permission of both the copyright
owner and the above publisher of this book.

*British Library Cataloguing-in-Publication Data*
A catalogue record for this book is available from the British Library.

Library of Congress Control Number: 2021951102

ISBN-13: 978-1-78527-954-6 (Hbk)
ISBN-10: 1-78527-954-8 (Hbk)

Cover credit: Smart city and IoT (Internet of Things) concept. ICT
(Information Communication Technology). By metamorworks/Shutterstock.com

This title is also available as an e-book.

# CONTENTS

# ILLUSTRATIONS

## Figures

## Tables

# CONTRIBUTORS

**Arindom Basu** is the founder and CEO of Digilytics (www.digilytics.ai), the easiest AI technology that enterprises can deploy. Throughout his 30-year professional career, Arindom has pioneered the adoption of disruptive technology in business and continues to do so with analytics and AI technology, through his Digilytics venture. Prior to this, Arindom spent a long and illustrious career in the corporate sector as a technology and business leader with Accenture and was a founding member of Infosys Consulting, and one of the leaders of the financial services unit of Infosys. Arindom has extensive global experience in advising clients across North America, Europe, and Asia with a specific focus on financial services.

**Maria Beamond** is an assistant professor at RMIT University, Australia. Before joining RMIT, she undertook two years postdoctoral scholar and research fellow at Pennsylvania State University. She obtained her PhD in management from the University of Queensland, Australia. Within human resource management, and international business fields, Maria's research interest covers international HRM, global talent management, artificial intelligence, corporate social responsibility, and emerging economies.

**Andrea Bencsik** is a professor at the University of Pannonia in Veszprém in Hungary and in J. Selye University in Slovakia. Her main research area is knowledge management and its connections with other processes, and knowledge-management system building in companies. She is the leader of an innovative research project which aims to work out new ideas on how artificial intelligence can support knowledge management and be viably connected with various processes in a company.

**Reetwija Chakraborty** is an experienced management consultant in financial services working at the intersection of UK mortgages and AI, driving digital transformation programmes at lenders. She is a trained economist from St. Xavier's College, Kolkata, a King's India (MSc) Scholar from King's College London, and a Young India Fellow.

**Wesley Doorsamy** received his PhD from the University of Witwatersrand, Johannesburg, South Africa. Currently he is serving as an associate professor at the Institute for Intelligent Systems, University of Johannesburg. He is a rated researcher with the National Research Foundation of South Africa.

**Sergio A. Escobar** is an investor across the United States and Canada with a diversified investment portfolio of companies ranging from B2B enterprises (leveraging artificial intelligence, big data, analytics and security) to B2C (leveraging IoT/wearables). Sergio has 15+ years of experience as a multiple times tech entrepreneur in aerospace, eCommerce, manufacturing, agtech and fintech. He's the global curator at Techstars Startup Digest in Artificial Intelligence. He has also been pioneering the Canadian investment scene by launching one of Canada's very first super angel funds.

**Margaret A. Goralski** holds a PhD in International Management. She is a professor of strategy at Quinnipiac University in Connecticut, USA. Goralski is an Albert Schweitzer Fellow; Chapter Chair of Academy of International Business US NE; VP of publications at *International Academy of Business Disciplines*; editor in chief of *Quarterly Review of Business Disciplines*; and UN PRME working group member on sustainability mindset. Her current research interests include global entrepreneurship and innovation: artificial intelligence, open cognition, and blockchain, and handling resultant unemployment from artificial intelligence. Goralski has authored/edited/co-edited multiple journal publications as well as contributed chapters on AI including 'Permissionless Evolution of Ethics – Artificial Intelligence in Business Strategy in the Artificial Intelligence Economy' with co-author Krystyna Górniak-Kocikowska.

**Krystyna Górniak-Kocikowska** has a PhD in Philosophy from Adam Mickiewicz University in Poznań, Poland, and an MA in Religious Studies from Temple University. She is a core faculty member at Charter Oak State College; Professor Emerita of Philosophy at Southern Connecticut State University; member of the editorial board of *Journal of Information, Communication & Ethics in Society*; member of the Research Center on Values in Emerging Science and Technology (RC-VEST); and an Albert Schweitzer Fellow. Her publications and conference presentations focus mainly on ethical and social issues generated by digital technology, especially artificial intelligence, philosophy of education, phenomenology, and interreligious dialogue.

She received several research and travel grants (among others, from the EU and from the Kościuszko Foundation).

**Faith Hatani** is Associate Professor of International Business in the Department of International Economics, Government and Business at Copenhagen Business School, Denmark. She has conducted research on the impact of foreign direct investment on economic development, and the governance of global value chains. Her current research focuses on the role of international business in sustainable development, responsible management, and the potentials and risks of new technologies in sustainability challenges.

**Akul Jain** is an experienced management consultant in consumer retail services working in the space of AI and consumer industries sector, consulting clients to infuse AI-driven transformational changes in their organizations. He has previously worked in Infosys Consulting for various clients across multiple geographies.

**Sergei O. Kuznetsov** graduated from Moscow Institute on Physics and Technology in 1985, obtained his doctorate degrees in theoretical computer science in 1990 and habilitation in 2002. He is currently the head of department of data analysis and AI at National Research University Higher School of Economics in Moscow and vice-president of the Russian Association for Artificial Intelligence.

**Oleg P. Kuznetsov**, graduated at the Mechanico-Mathematical Faculty (Mekhmat) of Moscow State University in 1965. He is doctor of science in automata theory and its applications. He heads a research laboratory at the Institute of Control Problems of Russian Academy of Science. Kuznetsov is the chair of the council of the Russian Association for Artificial Intelligence.

**Tshilidzi Marwala** is vice chancellor and principal of the University of Johannesburg. He was previously the deputy vice chancellor for Research and Internationalization as well as the dean of Engineering at the University of Johannesburg; professor of Electrical Engineering, the Carl and Emily Fuchs Chair of Systems and Control Engineering as well as the SARChI Chair of Systems Engineering at the University of the Witwatersrand.

**Alka Maurya** is professor at Amity International Business School, Amity University, Noida. She has over 19 years of experience in teaching, research, and consulting. Before joining Amity she worked with various trade promotion organizations where she worked on several research and consulting projects for the department of commerce, export promotion councils, commodity boards, MNCs, and MSMEs. She has published several research papers in leading national and international journals and has authored/edited/co-edited books in her area of specialization.

**Alan Montague's** research, experience, and publications are linked to skill/vocational shortages, government policies relating to the connections between education and industry, employment/education program policy development, and management and workforce planning sector. His research focus involves the investigation of the perspectives of leaders and managers, human resource management (HRM) professionals, and other industry-based professionals concerning the implications and planning responses to the impact of the Fourth Industrial Revolution on a range of industries, occupations, and workplaces and the transformation of jobs. His overall research is underpinned by academic commentary on the development of HRM practices that result in health and wellbeing generated within high-functioning work cultures.

**J. Mark Munoz** is a tenured Full Professor of International Business at Millikin University in Illinois, and a former visiting fellow at the Kennedy School of Government at Harvard University. He is a recipient of several awards including four Best Research Paper Awards, a Literary Award, an International Book Award, and the ACBSP Teaching Excellence Award among others. He was recognized as Distinguished Business Dean and was honored for Global Academic Excellence. Aside from top-tier journal publications, he has authored/edited/co-edited over 20 books including: *Handbook on the Geopolitics of Business, Global Business Intelligence, Economics of Cryptocurrencies, Handbook of Artificial Intelligence and Robotic Process Automation: Policy and Government Applications and Business Strategy in the Artificial Intelligence Economy.* He directs consulting projects worldwide in the areas of strategy formulation, business development, and international finance.

**Babu Sena Paul** received his PhD from the Indian Institute of Technology, Guwahati, India. From 2015 to 2018 he served as the head of department of Electrical and Electronic Engineering Technology, University of Johannesburg. Currently he is serving as the director of the Institute for Intelligent Systems at the University of Johannesburg.

**Diana Sciortino** is an investment analyst at BCF Ventures with diversified expertise in the areas of marketing, banking, venture capital, and law. She holds a BCom in accountancy from McGill University and is currently completing her LLB and JD degrees at the Faculty of Law. Diana has worked extensively with entrepreneurs, investors, portfolio companies, and AI superclusters for the sourcing of deals and identification of disruptive technologies. She is particularly well versed in the B2B enterprise software space, having explored developments in AI, big data, security and analytics in diverse industries.

**Rohit Sehgal** heads the India business of Digilytics. He is a career management and information technology consulting professional for over 30 years, with significant experience in consumer and manufacturing industries. Rohit has previously worked for Accenture and Tata Consultancy Services.

**Hassan Sirelkhatim** is a seasoned data scientist with demonstrated working experience in management consulting, and experience within multiple sectors including oil and  gas, manufacturing, government, retail and life sciences. Skilled in statistics, mathematical modeling, programming, and data analysis, Hassan is an engineering professional with a master's degree focused on bioinformatics from the University of Copenhagen. In his spare time, he enjoys delving into deep reinforcement learning and its applications to industry.

**Mehrdad S. Sharbaf** is an adjunct professor at multiple universities, including Loyola Marymount, California State University, Dominguez Hills, and California State University, Northridge. His background includes more than 20 years' experience in industry and academia, focusing on disciplines such as system integration, system engineering, information security, and total quality information security management. During his career, he has taught at multiple institutions, including various educational institutions such as the previously mentioned colleges, as well as CSU Long Beach, CSULA, and UCLA Extension. His research interests include quantum cryptography, quantum information processing, total quality information security management, and network design and integration.

**Kai-Ann D. Skeete** is Trade Research Fellow and Lecturer at the Shridath Ramphal Centre for International Trade Law, Policy and Services based at the University of the West Indies (UWI) Cave Hill Campus, Barbados. She is the author of several pieces of writing on the Caribbean governance and implementation efforts of regional integration. Her research interests include Caribbean regionalism, Latin American Foreign Policy, security studies and regional governance.

**Dan Wong** is a successful AI entrepreneur and tech executive with 15+ years' experience in China. As CEO of AI startup Rokid, Wong brought to market a cutting-edge home AI product in China that captured numerous domestic and international industry accolades, including CES Innovation Award 2016 and 2017. As an advisor to startups, Wong has been involved in the commercialization and application of AI across different industry sectors including manufacturing, supply chain, retail, and smart homes. Previous to this, Wong was a senior executive at Samsung and Nokia with P&L responsibility.

# Chapter 1

# INTRODUCTION

## J. Mark Munoz and Alka Maurya

Artificial intelligence (AI), or the foundation for the enhanced cognitive ability of machines, has grown by leaps and bounds over the years. It has refined and redefined business frameworks and has taken the notion of operational efficiency to an entirely new level.

As a result of AI, countless breakthroughs have taken place in many industries. Examples of industries that have benefited from AI include: healthcare (data-based diagnostic support), automotive (autonomous fleets for ride sharing), financial services (personalized financial planning), retail and consumer (personalized design and production), technology, communication and entertainment (media archiving and search), manufacturing (enhanced monitoring and auto correction), energy (smart meters), transport and logistics (autonomous trucking) and many more (PwC 2016).

AI has seeped into the day-to-day life of an individual as well, affecting the way they work, live and entertain themselves. Voice-based assistance systems like Siri and Alexa are common example of AI. Online shopping, web search, digital personal assistance, machine translation, smart homes, smart cities, infrastructure, logistics, education, driverless vehicles, and so forth are just few of the examples of integration of AI in commercial and personal applications. All the chapters in this book, contributed by authors from different parts of the world, provide an insight into the use of AI in all walks of life. AI is finding its way in each and every application at a pace one cannot imagine. By the time this book reaches the hands of the reader, there will be far more applications of AI than have been mentioned in this book.

AI can be characterized in at least five ways:

**Evolving:** Countless breakthroughs are taking place due to inroads in data retrieval and analysis, stronger computing power, and advances in algorithm creation. Advances in these areas, happening in tandem, accelerated the utilization of AI in organizations worldwide. However,

AI is still in its infancy stage. The field is young and is rapidly changing. It will continue to evolve further in the coming years.

**Global:** The ability of machines to process large quantities of data instantly also means that once applied it is not constrained by geographic boundaries. Data acquisition and analysis is borderless. Consequently, global trade is facilitated. Nesbitt (2017) indicated that AI impacts trade by (1) enabling supply chains, (2) creating efficiency in compliance software, (3) speeding up and creating better contracts, and (4) improving access to finance.

**Cross-functional:** AI is not a function of one corporate department. Business intelligence and cognitive output is valuable to all organizational units. AI is the means and the platform that can unify organizations.

**Value creator:** Innovation and efficiencies brought about by AI help firms create value in terms of cost and time savings, enhanced customer interaction, and product development. The key areas where AI can really make an impact include personalization, utility, data availability and time saving (PwC 2018).

**Time sensitive:** Given the rapid progress taking place worldwide as a result of AI, speed has become the basis of competitive advantage. The company with the best and the fastest AI architecture is poised to have an edge.

It is noteworthy that while AI has become a global phenomenon and likely to contribute about $15.7 trillion to the global economy by 2030 (PwC 2016), it is presently operating in silos. One still has to see countries collaborating as a community to address issues or help advance AI.

A corporate executive working in an AI department in the United States would likely not know the status of AI in China, Russia or even in neighboring Canada.

This book is an effort to engage the global community in a discussion on AI. Drawing from chapter contributions from experts in several countries, the book aims to provide snapshots of the status of AI in different parts of the world. The goal of this book is to help the reader understand similarities and differences in activities and policies in various countries. In the end, the authors hope that more collective discussions can be held to advance conversations on AI and to ensure that it progresses in the right direction.

While there are several operational and economic benefits brought about by AI, challenges exist. For instance, new technologies threaten about 40 percent of jobs in the United States and approximately two-thirds of those in the developing world (Gershon 2017). Only about 20 percent of organizations possess essential skills to succeed with AI technology (Rao 2017). Barriers that the field of AI has to overcome include: concerns over data protection and privacy, consumer trust and regulatory acceptance, building relevant technologies, managing the volume of unstructured data, optimizing supply chain and production systems, and securing resources for a potentially high investment requirement (PwC 2016).

On a policy level, governments have to frame technological conversations in new ways. With regard to AI, Mehr (2017) identified the need for governments to: (1) incorporate AI in their goals, (2) engage the citizenry, (3) build on existing resources, (4) consider data preparation, (5) manage ethical risks, and (6) strengthen employee potential.

The authors hope that this book is useful to the academic community by informing and providing opportunities for discourse on the topic of AI. It is also hoped that this book is valuable to the business community in general by offering ideas they can emulate from the cases in other countries. Finally, from the country cases, policy makers, consultants, international organizations and government officials can perhaps be inspired to pursue innovative and responsible pathways to AI. The authors hope that this book starts a global conversation that will positively impact the future of AI.

It is estimated that AI will contribute to about a 26 percent boost in the GDP of countries by 2030, and that 48 percent of this gain will come from product enhancements, stimulating consumer demand, greater product variety, increased personalization, attractiveness and affordability (PwC 2018). Some of the industries that will be disrupted due to AI are manufacturers of AI-powered chips, companies that are working to integrate Internet of Things (IoT) with AI, corporate business analytics, industries exploring application of facial recognition and automation with the help of AI technology and so on (Forbes 2019).

A report by International Data Corporation (IDC) predicts that spending on AI will reach around $110 billion by 2024 as compared to $50 billion in 2019 (WSJ 2020). Also the revenues from AI are expected to witness a five-year compounded annual growth rate (CAGR) of 17.1 percent to reach $300 billion in 2024 (ET 2020).

AI will transform modalities of business and governance in a profound way. This collage of ideas from all over the world provides a roadmap for exciting pathways ahead.

## References

ET (2020). Global AI market revenues to reach $156 billion in 2020: IDC. Accessed August 20, 2020. https://cio.economictimes.indiatimes.com/news/corporate-news/global-ai-market-revenues-to-reach-156-billion-in-2020-idc/77426114.

Forbes (2019). 5 top AI trends. Accessed March 5, 2020. https://www.forbes.com/sites/cog.nitiveworld/2019/04/25/5-top-ai-trends/#133f14206aa0.

Gershon, L. (2017). The automation resistant skills we should nurture. BBC. Accessed September 20, 2017. http://www.bbc.com/capital/story/20170726-the-automation-resistant-skills-we-should-nurture.

Mehr, H. (2017). Artificial intelligence: 6 steps government agencies can take. Accessed September 20, 2017. http://statescoop.com/artificial-intelligence-6-steps-government-agencies-can-take.

Nesbitt, J. (2017). 4 ways artificial intelligence is transforming trade. Accessed September 21, 2017. http://www.tradeready.ca/2017/topics/import-export-trade-management/4-ways-artificial-intelligence-transforming-trade/.

PwC (2016). Sizing the prize. PWC's global Artificial Intelligence study: Exploiting the AI revolution. Accessed September 21, 2017. https://www.pwc.com/gx/en/issues/data-and-analytics/publications/artificial-intelligence-study.html.

———. (2018). 2018 AI predictions. Accessed January 30, 2019. https://www.pwc.com/us/en/services/consulting/library/artificial-intelligence-predictions.html.

Rao, A. (2017). A strategist's guide to artificial intelligence. Strategy + business. Accessed September 20, 2017. https://www.strategy-business.com/article/A-Strategists-Guide-to-Artificial-Intelligence?gko=0abb5&utm_source=itw&utm_medium=20170523&utm_campaign=respB.

WSJ (2020). World-wide AI spending expected to double in next four years. Accessed August 25, 2020. https://www.wsj.com/articles/world-wide-ai-spending-expected-to-double-in-next-four-years-11598520600.

# Chapter 2

# ARTIFICIAL INTELLIGENCE IN THE UNITED STATES

Margaret A. Goralski and Krystyna Górniak-Kocikowska

What was once a figment of imagination in the minds of science fiction writers is now a ubiquitous reality in the United States of America. There are already various AI-endowed products in the market including: Garmin's "auto-land" which can manage aircraft speed and engine performance or even descend towards the nearest airport and land a plane in case of a medical emergency (Pasztor 2020), and Clean Air, a technology that monitors and fixes air quality through fresh air, tempered, filtered and treated with ultraviolet light (McLaughlin 2020). In addition, primary healthcare is moving to a team of health-care professionals whose direct compensation is linked to keeping patients healthy by uploading data from home-monitoring equipment (Landro 2020). There are also trends for the future that are more indicative of science fiction: building a better athlete through tweaked brain circuits, culturing performance-boosting bacteria, and enhancing strength, speed and endurance by altering genes (Hotz and Hand 2020); seeking romance and friendship from artificial intelligence (AI) in the form of a chatbot for conversation during times of quarantine (Olson 2020); and producing meat in bioreactor tanks from animal cells rather than raising and slaughtering chickens, cattle and hogs (Bunge 2020).

As AI continues to develop, governments and practitioners must ensure that AI-enabled systems can work effectively with people and hold ideals that remain consistent with human values and aspirations; but this will not be easy. Increased attention has been drawn to these challenges and many believe that AI will create a better and wiser path forward for humankind. However, realistically one of the greatest challenges will be the risks involved for all citizens as AI continues to evolve and increase its impact on the workforce and society. The world is ever more competitive, and the underlying premise is that governments, industries and educational institutions that are ahead of the

AI curve will reap the benefits of technological breakthroughs. The United States, in addition to many other advanced nations, aim to be at the forefront of these breakthroughs. This chapter will explore the good, the bad and the ugly, and then perhaps the beautiful of AI in the United States.

In October 2016, the Executive Office of the President of the United States and the National Science and Technology Council Committee on Technology, understanding the relevance of AI in opening new markets worldwide and creating new opportunities, commissioned a document titled 'Preparing for the Future of Artificial Intelligence'.

In February 2019, the Executive Office of the President of the United States and Office of Science and Technology Policy initiated the American Artificial Intelligence Initiative—the US strategy to promote American leadership in AI (Artificial Intelligence for... 2019; American Artificial Intelligence... 2020). The initiative focuses governmental resources to support innovation in AI to increase prosperity, enhance the quality of life for people of the United States and improve its economic and national security. The strategy emphasizes the following:

- Investment in AI research and development;
- Access to Federal AI data, models and resources;
- Removal of barriers to innovation in AI;
- Apprenticeships, skill-building programs and STEM (science, technology, engineering and mathematics) education for future generations of workers;
- Promotion of a supportive international environment for American AI innovation;
- Building AI for government missions and services that will incorporate the values and trust of the American people.

For fiscal year (FY) 2020, the Networking and Information Technology Research and Development (NITRE) Program provided an agency-by-agency report of US unclassified, nondefense investments in AI R&D totaling $973.5 million. For FY 2021, the proposed budget included a major increase over FY 2020, with plans to double government nondefense spending on AI by 2022 (American Artificial Intelligence... 2020, 4–5). This amount of US funding for nondefense spending is historically unprecedented, but deemed necessary if government, industry and academia are going to work together on AI initiatives, especially initiatives that address specific societal needs that will not lead to commercial profits.

According to Anand Rao, global leader of AI, and Gerard Verweij, global and US data and analytics leader, PricewaterhouseCoopers (PwC), a multi-national professional services network, global gross domestic product (GDP) could be up to 14 percent higher by 2030 as a result of implementing AI, which would be equivalent to an additional $15.7 trillion, making it the largest commercial opportunity in a rapidly changing economy.

Although there are many different definitions of AI, for this chapter we will use the Rao and Verweij (n.d.) definition: "AI is a collective term for computer systems that can sense their environment, think, learn, and take action in response to what they're sensing and their objectives" (p. 2). This is an interesting definition because it focuses on strong AI, and places AI in a human domain. The possibilities based on a combination of AI and humans working together present countless additional variations of intelligences, which will be explored minimally in this chapter.

Notably, Rao and Verweij consider one of the questions that has also been raised by the US government, computer ethicists and philosophers—how to build AI in a responsible and transparent way such that it will gain or maintain the confidence of citizens and economic stakeholders and allow people to trust AI and AI decisions. In order for this to occur, AI and its developers would have to allow people to know how AI itself works and provide sufficient guarantees on the safety, security and resiliency of its operation. Further, AI development would need to emphasize mechanisms that assist human users to understand the reasoning behind AI outputs, along with procedures to evaluate, test, validate and verify its performance. Transparency would depend on a human understanding of the data utilized to train AI systems and its veracity and fitness for the application where it is being used.

In some ways, we can see from the research of the US government, Rao and Verweij, and others that there are great benefits to developing and utilizing AI for future advances in economic growth and national security. In times of worldwide pandemics like COVID-19, AI becomes even more important to keep societies running and people in touch with each other. As citizens became isolated and quarantined, education from elementary through university levels needed to continue at least until the end of the term. In healthcare, technology and digitalization were utilized to track breakouts of the virus, hospital bed optimization and case versus death rates among various populations within a particular area and worldwide. For industry, governmental mandates dictated and superseded decisions that would ordinarily be made by organizational executives under crisis situations.

Ayanna Howard, Linda J. and Mark C. Smith Professor and Chair of the School of Interactive Computing in the College of Computing at Georgia Institute of Technology, and Jason Borenstein, director of graduate research ethics programs and associate director of the Center for Ethics and Technology within the School of Public Policy and Office of Graduate Studies at Georgia Tech (2020) state that many of the concerns of society related to discomfort with the use of AI fearing takeover of jobs previously performed by humans seem to have diminished as technology's perceived value during COVID-19 outweighed its preconceived downsides. Howard and Borenstein (2020) question what will happen when humans want their jobs back, similar to the retrenchment of men upon return from the Second World War to a job market that had been taken over by females whose productivity was as high as their male counterparts (Kossoudji and Dresser 1992). Will there be a retrenchment of humans after this pandemic, or will AI become a more viable alternative?

As organizational leaders delve more deeply into the opportunities and probability of AI, they should also be aware of the biases that still exist in AI and the potential for algorithms to assist in decisions that include life and death situations, for instance, in the day-to-day operations of hospitals and healthcare facilities. The US Defense Advanced Research Projects Agency (DARPA) is creating approaches to AI that are not as reliant on large-scale data in hopes of alleviating the technical and ethical shortcomings of purely data-driven AI (American Artificial Intelligence... 2020). Privacy concerns in data collection and accuracy of that data are also a concern as AI becomes more prolific. Once surveillance measures are put in place, even during times of crisis, it will be difficult to eradicate those powers from governments, organizations and others that have access to the information (Howard and Borenstein 2020). Organizational challenges to prepare employees for additional use of AI will require leaders to think, act and make decisions in new ways (Brown et al. 2019).

At the World Economic Forum in Davos, Switzerland, 2020 was the year for commitment to an initiative titled the "Reskilling Revolution" where governments and organizations pledged "to reskill and upskill one billion people across the world by 2030" (Gratton 2020, para. 3). Lynda Gratton, a professor of management practice at London Business School and director of the school's Human Resource Strategy in Transforming Companies program, questioned why organizations, governments or even workers would want to be reskilled or upskilled. She likened the reskilling revolution to climate change with everyone knowing that something must to be done but wondering what the motivations are to change. She states that in order for these pledges to be realized incentives would need to be attached to those pledges. Gratton set forth four incentives: fiscal incentives, fiscal support, reporting incentives and signaling incentives, but there was no consensus that those incentives would be put in place (Gratton 2020). They are just theoretical.

With AI, there will be massive industry disruptions. Rao and Verweij (n.d.) view these disruptions as positive, signaling a consumer revolution that will open the doors for new entrants to drive innovation and new business models for established businesses to gain additional customer insights. But at the opposite end of the spectrum, there will be a shift in the job market, and for some businesses, humans will no longer need to apply (Goralski and Gorniak-Kocikowska 2018; Grey 2014).

David McCann (2019), citing a PwC AI predictions survey of 1062 respondents, notes that corporate executives are rethinking their plans to implement AI solutions in 2020 with only 4 percent of respondents planning to deploy AI enterprise-wide compared to 20 percent in 2019. While McCann highlights five reasons why corporate executives are rethinking AI deployment, we will concentrate on the perceived risks due to bias in algorithms and/or AI-powered "deepfakes" (a form of artificial intelligence called deep learning to make images of fake events that purport to be the real thing) (Sample 2020) to name just two of the alleged 'darker sides' of AI. Perhaps the more critical risk of deepfakes is the one stated by Professor Lilian Edwards, a leading expert in internet law at Newcastle University, "The problem may not be so much the faked reality as the fact that real reality becomes plausibly deniable" (Edwards in Sample 2020, para. 19). This then leads one to not know if something is true or fake, and more importantly the two realities blend together until information lies somewhere in limbo between true and false. Benjamin Cheatham, Kia Javanmardian and Hamid Samandari (2019), senior partners at McKinsey and Company, cite additional risks by adding loss of human life based on a wrong diagnosis of an AI medical algorithm or compromised national security if adverse information is fed into military AI systems. These new AI risks present significant challenges to governmental and organizational leaders. They are much more complex than the risks that most leaders are historically prepared to meet.

The most optimistic outlook is perhaps for mutual learning between humans and AI (Rao et al. 2017; Saenz et al. 2020). As AI continues to gain intellectually, its values are shifting and it is becoming more sentient by acquiring more human characteristics and experiences, for example, creativity, thinking and problem-solving. However, as introduced in some of our earlier publications, as AI becomes more adept at thinking and problem-solving, humans are using these qualities less and are therefore becoming less proficient during this same time period as we transition into an era of transference of intelligence (Goralski and Górniak-Kocikowska 2018, 2019, 2020).

We began this chapter by stating that AI is ubiquitous in the United States. We walked you through some of the good—more nondefense investments in AI R&D by the US government, 14 percent increase in GDP by 2030 as a result of AI (equivalent to an additional $15.7 trillion), the need for development to emphasize mechanisms that assist human users to understand the reasoning behind AI outputs, and the ability of AI to keep us connected so education and the economy could continue during COVID-19 or a similar crisis. We talked about some of the bad—the risks involved in AI taking over jobs currently held by humans, leaving humans out of the loop in decision-making processes, the accuracy of data collection and mistakes that could be made. Then we touched on the ugly—deepfakes and the fact that real reality could become plausibly deniable, bias in algorithms, security risks and loss of life due to AI medical or military decisions. And, finally, we promised the beautiful. AI is opening up academia, industry and governments to new ways of thinking, new ways of seeing and new innovative opportunities. The silos in academia are breaking down and we can write from a business perspective with a philosophical background why we are where we are and how we can achieve new innovation and greatness. We have become more transparent in human interactions and we are now asking the same from our AI counterparts. Each day is a new beginning. We do not know where our future will be, but in reality, humans have never been able to accurately predict their futures. We stand on the brink of all possibilities.

## References

American Artificial Intelligence Initiative: Year One Annual Report (2020). The White House Executive Office of the President of the United States and Office of Science and Technology Policy. Accessed May 26, 2020. https://www.nitrd.gov/nitrdgroups/images/c/c1/American-AI-Initiative-One-Year-Annual-Report.pdf.

Artificial Intelligence for the American People (2019). The White House Executive Office of the President of the United States and Office of Science and Technology Policy. Accessed May 26, 2020. https://trumpwhitehouse.archives.gov/ai/.

Brown, S., Gandhi, D., Herring, L., and Puri, A. (2019). The analytics academy: Bridging the gap between human and artificial intelligence. *McKinsey Quarterly.* Accessed January 29, 2020. https://www.mckinsey.com/business-functions/mckinsey-analytics/our-insights/the-analytics-academy-bridging-the-gap-between-human-and-artificial-intelligence.

Bunge, J. (2020). California company's cell-grown chicken gets nod from Singapore. *Wall Street Journal.* Accessed January 23, 2021. https://www.wsj.com/articles/california-companys-cell-grown-chicken-gets-nod-from-singapore-11606973635#:~:text=California%20food%20company%20Eat%20Just,aims%20to%20revolutionize%20meat%20production.&text=The%20agency%20said%20the%20meat,in%20Eat%20Just's%20nuggets%20product.

Cheatham, B., Javanmardian, K., and Samandari, H. (2019). Confronting the risks of artificial intelligence. *McKinsey Quarterly.* Accessed April 25, 2020. https://www.mckinsey.com/business-functions/mckinsey-analytics/our-insights/confronting-the-risks-of-artificial-intelligence.

Goralski, M. A., and Górniak-Kocikowska, K. 2018). Permissionless evolution of ethics—artificial intelligence. In J. Mark Munoz and Al Naqvi (eds.), *Business Strategy in an Artificial Intelligence Economy*, pp. 69–78. New York: Business Expert Press.

Goralski, M. A., and Górniak-Kocikowska, K. (2019). Education in the era of artificial intelligence: The willingness to listen as a new pedagogical challenge. *ETHOS,* 32(1): 152–98. (Originally published in Polish.)

Goralski, M. A., and Górniak-Kocikowska, K. (2020). Handling resultant unemployment from artificial intelligence. In J. Mark Munoz and Al Naqvi (eds.), *Handbook of Artificial Intelligence and Robotic Process Automation: Policy and Government Applications*, pp. 67–76. London: Anthem Press.

Gratton, L. (2020). Davos 2020: The upskilling agenda. *MIT Sloan Management Review*. Accessed April 25, 2020. https://sloanreview.mit.edu/article/davos-2020-the-upskilling-agenda/.

Grey, C. G. P. (2014). Humans need not apply. *YouTube*. Accessed April 29, 2020. https://www.youtube.com/watch?v=7Pq-S557XQU.

Hotz, R. L., and Hand, K. (2020). How to build a better Athlete. *Wall Street Journal*. Accessed April 29, 2020. https://www.wsj.com/articles/the-athlete-of-tomorrow-11583433479.

Howard, A., and Borenstein, J. (2020). AI, robots, and ethics in the age of COVID-19. *MIT Sloan Management Review*. Accessed June 27, 2020. https://sloanreview.mit.edu/article/ai-robots-and-ethics-in-the-age-of-covid-19/.

Kossoudji, S. A., and Dresser, L. J. (1992). Working class Rosies: Women industrial workers during World War II. *Journal of Economic History*, 52(2): 431–46. Accessed March 13, 2020. https://www.jstor.org/stable/2123119?seq=1.

Landro, L. (2020). The doctor won't see you now. Accessed October 15, 2020. https://www.wsj.com/articles/the-new-doctors-appointment-11599662314.

McCann, D. (2019). 5 Priorities for moving ahead with AI in 2020. *CFO*. Accessed April 25, 2020. https://www.cfo.com/artificial-intelligence/2019/12/5-priorities-for-moving-ahead-with-ai-in-2020/.

McLaughlin, K. (2020). Clean air: The next luxury apartment perk. *Wall Street Journal*. Accessed December 12, 2020. https://www.cfo.com/artificial-intelligence/2019/12/5-priorities-for-moving-ahead-with-ai-in-2020/.

Olson, P. (2020). My girlfriend is a chatbot. *Wall Street Journal*. Accessed December 12, 2020. https://www.wsj.com/articles/my-girlfriend-is-a-chatbot-11586523208.

Pasztor, A. (2020). Press a button and this plane lands itself. *Wall Street Journal*. Accessed December 12, 2020. https://www.wsj.com/articles/press-a-button-and-this-plane-lands-itself-11595044800.

Preparing for the Future of Artificial Intelligence. (2016). Executive Office of the President, National Science and Technology Council, and Committee on Technology. Accessed July 20, 2020. https://obamawhitehouse.archives.gov/sites/default/files/whitehouse_files/microsites/ostp/NSTC/preparing_for_the_future_of_ai.pdf.

Rao, A., Lieberman, M., and Bothun, D. (2017). Bot.me: A revolutionary partnership—how artificial intelligence is pushing man and machine closer together. Consumer Intelligence Series. *PwC*. Accessed April 27, 2020. https://www.pwc.com/it/it/publications/assets/docs/PwC_botme-booklet.pdf.

Rao, A. S., and Verweij, G. (n.d.). Sizing the prize: What's the real value of AI for your business and how can you capitalise? *PwC*. Accessed May 26, 2020. https://www.pwc.com/gx/en/issues/analytics/assets/pwc-ai-analysis-sizing-the-prize-report.pdf.

Saenz, M. J., Revilla, E., and Simón, C. (2020). Designing AI systems with human-machine teams. *MIT Sloan Management Review*. Accessed April 26, 2020. https://sloanreview.mit.edu/article/designing-ai-systems-with-human-machine-teams/.

Sample, I. (2020). What are deepfakes—and how can you spot them? *The Guardian*. Accessed March 25, 2020. https://www.theguardian.com/technology/2020/jan/13/what-are-deepfakes-and-how-can-you-spot-them.

# Chapter 3

# ARTIFICIAL INTELLIGENCE IN CANADA

Sergio A. Escobar and Diana Sciortino

## Introduction

Over the past 30 years, Canada has been able to support the deployment of the world's largest and most powerful artificial intelligence (AI) science community by investing rapidly in machine learning and deep learning research. Today, Canada's knowledge of AI has spread around the world.

## Canada: A Global Artificial Intelligence Hub

Since the proliferation of modern AI in the 1950s, Canada has maintained its status as a global innovation hub in AI by implementing decisive national programs with long-term impacts. Canada continues to provide critical support to AI development and has quickly become a host nation for some of the most brilliant scientific minds in machine learning and deep learning. However, without a robust business-driven ecosystem taking those research discoveries into a commercial phase, Canada faces the challenge of not effectively benefitting from the industrial implementation of AI. As policymakers continue to support nationwide research programs, they remain committed to crystallizing the development of an AI-driven ecosystem.

### *Understanding Canada's Research-Led AI Model*

*Building the Foundations: Creation of CIFAR*

In the early 1980s, Japan launched an innovative research program on "fifth-generation" computing systems,[1] which integrated AI. This initiative spurred the launch of other research programs elsewhere in the world as part of an important step in technological advancement. In 1982, Canada created the Canadian Institute for Advanced Research (CIFAR) with the purpose of promoting knowledge breakthroughs, innovation and notable advances within the Canadian research community. In fact, in 1983, CIFAR launched the AI & Society Program, a national program, which was one of the world's first research programs specialized in AI. Decades later, it remains a foundational program for Canada's current status as both an AI hub and research leader.[2]

*Attracting Global Talent: The Godfathers of Artificial Intelligence*

In the late 1980s, funding for research projects in AI was dramatically cut worldwide. Regarded as the "AI Winter," CIFAR provided critical support to scientists in the field of AI. As a result, Canada retained its scientific talent, while attracting international brilliant minds such as Dr. Geoffrey Hinton from the United Kingdom, a recognized pioneer in deep learning. During his time in Toronto, Dr. Hinton developed deep neural networks, considered the most powerful form of machine learning. His research attracted other specialists to relocate to Canada for their research, including a French-born computer scientist, Dr. Yann LeCun. Dr. LeCun is now recognized for his research in computer vision and machine learning and acts as the chief AI scientist at Facebook. Similarly, French-born Dr. Yoshua Bengio relocated to Canada and later established the Montreal Institute of Learning Algorithms (Mila) which specializes in neural networks and deep learning. In 2018, the Association for Computing Machinery (ACM) granted the famous Turing Award to Dr. Yoshua Bengio, Dr. Geoffrey Hinton and Dr. Yann LeCun. This honour is bestowed to individuals who have contributed to a conceptual and engineering breakthrough, particularly in the areas of neural networks and computing. Today, the afore-mentioned award recipients are widely recognized as the "Godfathers of Artificial Intelligence."[3]

*Strengthening the Foundations: Canada's AI National Strategy—a World's First*

In 2017, Canada became the first country in the world to announce a national strategy for AI and appointed CIFAR to lead the US$125 million-dollar Pan-Canadian Artificial Intelligence Strategy.[4] The national strategy aimed to limit brain drain and promoted efforts to attract more brilliant AI minds to Canada. Through the funding of research centers, the number of outstanding AI researchers and skilled graduates in Canada con-currently increased. As nation's leaders began raising concerns over the responsible use of AI technologies, CIFAR was mandated to develop global leadership in the economic, ethical, political and legal implications of advancements in AI.

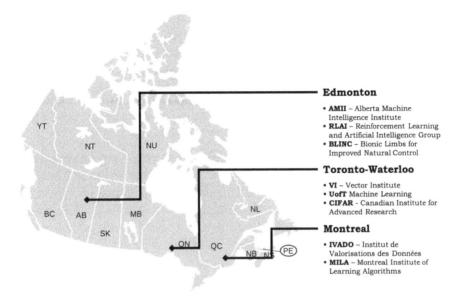

**Figure 3.1** Canada map: AI international perspectives
*Source:* Produced by the author using a main blank map of Canada from Wikipedia Commons (2009)

*Modelling Canada's AI Research Ecosystem: Deep Research*

While the Canadian government deployed great efforts to develop specialized AI research units in all major cities, through the 2017 Pan-Canadian Artificial Intelligence Strategy, Canada prioritized three main hubs for research in AI, which include Montreal, Toronto and Edmonton (see Figure 3.1).

Montreal Hub
Two academic institutions, University of Montreal and McGill University, are responsible for the research institutions known as Institut de Valorisations des Données (IVADO) and the Mila. One of the representatives of the Montreal AI research community is Dr. Yoshua Bengio. While retaining his professorship, Dr. Bengio acts as founder and scientific director of both IVADO and Mila research centers.

Toronto-Waterloo Hub
Headquartered in Toronto, CIFAR is the leading Canadian organization responsible for the Pan-Canadian Artificial Intelligence Strategy for research and talent. The city hosts two main research centers, including the Vector Institute (VI) and the Machine Learning Group at the University of

Toronto. In the greater Toronto region, the University of Waterloo launched the newly created Waterloo Artificial Intelligence Institute. One of the main representatives of the Toronto-Waterloo AI research community is Dr. Geoffrey Hinton. While retaining his professorship, Dr. Hinton joined Google Brain in 2013 as a distinguished research scientist. He currently acts as chief scientific advisor for the Vector Institute.

Edmonton Hub
The University of Alberta hosts the three main research centers, which include the Alberta Machine Intelligence Institute (AMII), the Reinforcement Learning and Artificial Intelligence Group (RLAI) and the Bionic Limbs for Improved Natural Control (BLINC). One of the main representatives of the Edmonton AI research community is Dr. Richard Sutton, a scientist born in the United States and who is considered the "Father of Reinforcement Learning." While retaining his professorship, Dr. Sutton joined Google Deepmind in 2017 as a distinguished research scientist and cofounder of its Edmonton office.

### *Developing Canada's Business-Led AI Model*

*Designing Canada's AI Business Ecosystem: Scale AI SuperCluster*

According to McKinsey, AI could enable US$13 trillion in additional economic activity by 2030, which is representative of an additional 1.2 percent growth in Canadian GDP.[5] While Canada has spent close to forty years funding AI research, policymakers are now tasked with transferring such technologies to the Canadian industrial complex. As such, in 2018, the government of Canada launched the Innovation SuperCluster Initiative, where funding from the Canadian government is matched by contributions from the private sector.[6] Among all superclusters, Montreal-based Scale AI is set to exceed US$500 million in direct investments in AI by 2030. The expected outcome, over a period of ten years, is to add US$16.5 billion to Canada's GDP while generating 16,000 new high-skilled jobs[7].

Training of an AI-Driven Workforce
The advent of AI in the private sector will undoubtedly create new jobs for highly skilled individuals. However, as corporations digitize and automate their legacy processes, AI will displace large segments of the Canadian workforce. As such, the government of Canada has also mandated the Scale AI SuperCluster to support professional development in the field of AI. By 2023, the expected outcome is to train 20,000 professionals in the Province of Quebec and 25,000 in the rest of Canada.

Industrial Adoption of Artificial Intelligence

The presence of highly skilled AI scientists and researchers has generated a flourishing tech ecosystem within the Canadian landscape. This pool of talent has attracted the attention of large American corporations and venture capital funds, resulting in an important influx of investments and acquisitions of Canadian ventures. In an effort to avoid a tech-drain to the United States, the government of Canada has mandated Scale AI SuperCluster to financially support the implementation and transfer of technologies from Canadian start-ups to Canadian corporations, targeting the adoption and commercialization of AI for supply chains.

## Responsible Development of Artificial Intelligence

Given the novelty of AI and the wide-scale applicability of its technologies, regulatory frameworks are necessary to safeguard against unprecedented risks. Without a robust regulatory framework, machine learning technologies have the potential to perpetuate existing stereotypes. As policymakers explore diverse uses of AI in programs and services, they are mindful of the ancillary impacts on ethics and fairness.

### Recent Regulatory Trends

*Toward a Learning Community: CIFAR's AI & Society Program*

Through CIFAR's AI & Society Program, researchers, policymakers and practitioners alike benefit from interdisciplinary training and informative workshops. AI Future Policy Labs are hosted by industry experts across various sectors of government, law, ethics, healthcare and academia, designed to provoke meaningful discussion. By supporting both national and international initiatives, CIFAR's AI & Society Program challenged the research community to address the timely and increasingly complex particularities of AI use and development.

*Montreal as Pioneer: Declaration for Responsible Development of Artificial Intelligence*

With growing concern over the use of AI, in December 2018, the University of Montreal, in partnership with the Fonds de Recherches du Quebec, launched the Montreal Declaration for Responsible Development of Artificial Intelligence[8]. The Declaration set out to address the ethical and moral challenges that come with the continued development of AI, encouraging a broad dialogue between the government, industry experts and the public. A key objective of the Declaration was to identify the ethical principles and values applicable to the fields of digital technology and AI that promote public interests and social progress. In addition to providing recommendations as to the fulfillment of a responsible digital transition, the Declaration articulated an overarching commitment to the following principles: well-being, autonomy, privacy, solidarity, democratic participation, equity, diversity inclusion, responsibility and sustainable development.[9]

### Federal Call to Action: Directive on Automated Decision-Making

In response to an effort to utilize AI to facilitate administrative decision-making of in-service delivery, the government of Canada issued a Directive on Automated Decision-Making in April 2019.[10] Compatible with core administrative law principles of transparency, accountability, legality, due process and procedural fairness, the Directive set out to support the proliferation of AI within the Canadian sphere without compromising public reporting, verifiability and auditing requirements. While the Directive does not extend to the private sector, it is applicable to all automated decision-making systems used by the federal government to provide services or administrative functions to external clients.

### Guiding Principles for AI Regulation

In an effort to ensure the effective and ethical use of AI, the Canadian government has made a pledge to operate as a function of five guiding principles.[11] First, a commitment toward proper understanding and measurement of the impacts of AI through the development and sharing of tools and approaches. Second, a commitment toward total transparency regarding the use of AI, particularly an articulation of user necessity and public benefit. Third, a commitment toward providing meaningful explanations and justifications for AI decision making, all the while offering opportunities to review results and challenge governmental decisions. Fourth, a commitment to be as open as possible with respect to sharing code, training data and other relevant information with due regard for the protection of personal information, system integration, national security and defense. Finally, a commitment toward the provision of sufficient training such that government employees developing and using AI solutions possess the responsible design, function and implementation skills needed to ameliorate AI-based public services.

*Artificial Impact Assessments: An Ethical Solution to AI Concerns*

In conjunction with the Directive on Automated Decision-Making, the Canadian government designed an Algorithmic Impact Assessment[12] (AIA) questionnaire to help assess and mitigate the risks associated with automated decision systems through appropriate governance and accountability. With the goal of building a responsible and transparent solution, the AIA provides designers with a measure to evaluate AI solutions from an ethical and human perspective, balancing economic interests with environmental sustainability and social benefit causes. The AIA includes ways to measure potential impacts to the public and outlines appropriate courses of action such as behavioral monitoring and algorithm assessments. The impact assessments seek to ensure ethical AI use by supporting informed decision-making and the protection of societal concerns, facilitating compliance with legal and other regulatory requirements, improving public confidence and constituting evidence of due diligence.[13]

## Legislative Backstory, Political Pressures and Canadian Governance

*G7 Multistakeholder Conference on Artificial Intelligence*

Two hundred participants including the greatest thinkers in civil society and academia attended the G7 Multistakeholder Conference on Artificial Intelligence,[14] held in Montréal in December of 2018. Given that emerging technologies do not take on a single form, a one-size-fits-all approach to AI regulation was deemed insufficient. Instead, the proposed course of action encouraged international leaders to adopt a human-centric, responsible and ethical approach to AI development. Canada has exerted efforts to maintain its position as an AI leader by partnering with other nations that share similar goals and implementation strategies. On March 28, 2018, Prime Minister Justin Trudeau, in partnership with French President Emmanuel Macron, announced a joint task force to guide the launch of the International Panel on AI (IPAI). The IPAI is an organization that brings together global AI experts in an attempt to collaborate and coordinate on AI policy development—an important step toward ensuring ethical AI advancement.[15]

*International Initiatives: GPAI and ICEMAI Explained*

The Global Partnership on Artificial Intelligence (GPAI) connects countries and experts across various disciplines and stakeholder groups to support the

development of AI. In collaboration with the GPAI and the French government, the International Centre of Expertise in Montréal for the Advancement
on Artificial Intelligence (ICEMAI) was founded to support responsible AI
governance, particularly as it relates to human rights, inclusion and diversity.
Led by Montréal International, ICEMAI works closely with the Government
of Canada's Advisory Council on AI, Forum IA Québec and the International
Observatory on the Societal Impacts of AI and Digital Technologies.[16] The
creation of GPAI and ICEMAI exemplify Canada's dedication to innovation,
commitment to community and international leadership within the AI sphere.

*Recent Developments—UNESCO World Consultation*

The Québec government recently granted funding to the Mila, to organize
UNESCO's global online consultation on AI ethics. Launched on July 8, 2020,
the research institute rallies the deep learning expertise of over five hundred
esteemed researchers. In a quest toward scientific advancement, innovation
and AI development, the consultation will bring together some of the brightest
minds to deliver a Recommendation on the Ethics of AI to be submitted for
approval to UNESCO by 2021.[17] In partnership with Algora Lab, Mila is
slated to organize the deliberative component of the initiative to include 60
online workshops in 25 countries, providing both capacity and knowledge to
UNESCO's global consultation efforts. As our nation continues to dabble in
the areas of algorithmic decision-making, Canada continues to recognize the
social potential of AI on job creation, international trade and social services.

## Conclusion

While AI has undoubtedly had a positive impact on the lives of humans,
it equally poses a number of challenges to governments, businesses and
society at large. As a world leader in AI, Canada faces moral, social and ethical obligations to lead the responsible development of this powerful new
technology.

## Notes

1   B. R. Gaines, "Perspectives on fifth generation computing," *Oxford Surveys in Information Technology*, 1 (1984): 1–53.
2   T. Dutton, "Building an AI world: Report on national and regional AI strategies," CIFAR (2018): 5–13.
3   Association for Computing Machinery, "Fathers of the deep learning revolution receive ACM A.M. Turing Award." Accessed March 27, 2019. https://www.acm.org/media-center/2019/march/turing-award-2018.

4  CIFAR, "CIFAR pan-Canadian Artificial Intelligence Strategy" (2017–20). Accessed July 16, 2021. https://www.cifar.ca/ai/pan-canadian-artificial-intelligence-strategy.

5  J. Bughin et al.," Notes from the AI frontier: Modeling the impact of AI on the world economy." September 4, 2018. https://www.mckinsey.com/featured-insights/artificial-intelligence/notes-from-the-ai-frontier-modeling-the-impact-of-ai-on-the-world-economy#.

6  Government of Canada, "Innovation Superclusters Initiative." September 4, 2018. https://www.ic.gc.ca/eic/site/093.nsf/eng/home.

7  Scale AI, "About us—FAQ," (2018–20). Accessed July 16, 2021. https://www.scaleai.ca/about-us/faq/.

8  University of Montreal, "Montreal Declaration for Responsible Development of Artificial Intelligence: A participatory process." Accessed March 11, 2017. https://nouvelles.umontreal.ca/en/article/2017/11/03/montreal-declaration-for-a-responsible-development-of-artificial-intelligence/.

9  Declaration de Montreal: IA Responsible, "Official launch of the Montreal Declaration for Responsible Development of Artificial Intelligence." Accessed December 5, 2018. https://ai.quebec/wp-content/uploads/sites/2/2018/12/News-release_Launch_Montreal_Declaration_AI-04_12_18.pdf.

10  Government of Canada, "Directive on automated decision-making." Accessed February 5, 2019. https://www.tbs-sct.gc.ca/pol/doc-eng.aspx?id=32592.

11  Government of Canada, "Our guiding principles." Accessed September 9, 2019. https://www.canada.ca/en/government/system/digital-government/modern-emerging-technologies/responsible-use-ai.html#tocl.

12  Government of Canada, "Algorithmic impact assessment." Accessed May 31, 2019. https://www.canada.ca/en/government/system/digital-government/modern-emerging-technologies/responsible-use-ai/algorithmic-impact-assessment.html.

13  *Medium*, "The government of Canada's algorithmic impact assessment: Take two." Accessed August 7, 2018. https://medium.com/@supergovernance/the-government-of-canadas-algorithmic-impact-assessment-take-two-8a22a87acf6f.

14  Government of Canada, "G7 Summit Conference 2018." Accessed December 6, 2018. https://www.ic.gc.ca/eic/site/133.nsf/vwapj/EN_MSC-Final-Report.pdf/$file/EN_MSC-Final-Report.pdf.

15  Innovation, Science and Economic Development Canada, "Canada and France work with international community to support responsible use of artificial intelligence." Accessed May 16, 2019. https://www.canada.ca/en/innovation-science-economic-development/news/2019/05/canada-and-france-work-with-international-community-to-support-responsible-use-of-artificial-intelligence.html.

16  Montreal International, "The global partnership on artificial intelligence officially launched." Accessed June 15, 2020. https://www.montrealinternational.com/en/news/the-global-partnership-on-artificial-intelligence-officially-launched/.

17  Mila, "Global consultation on AI ethics: Mila receives financial assistance from Quebec government." Accessed July 8, 2020. https://mila.quebec/en/global-consultation-on-ai-ethics-mila-receives-financial-assistance-from-quebec-government/.

# Chapter 4

# THE MAD MAX INTERCEPTOR EXPERIENCE IN THE UK: ARTIFICIAL INTELLIGENCE IN MORTGAGES

Arindom Basu, Hassan Sirelkhatim and
Reetwija Chakraborty

## Introduction

> Owning a home is a keystone of wealth […] both financial affluence and emotional security.
>
> —Suze Orman ('Thoughts for Success', 2010)

The above words have never been truer than in a world rendered uncertain and chaotic with a virus on the loose. With rigid social distancing protocols established to combat the pandemic, the meaning of home ownership is transcending connotations of just 'financial affluence'. For most, mortgages are now the most vital pillar of finance.

The mortgage market in the UK strives to continuously reinvent itself to meet the changing demands of its growing and evolving aspirational customer base. You may be privy to the pre-screening methods to assess the viability of a loan that have been in vogue for quite a while. Alternatively, you might even be using credit scoring vendors to check your general eligibility for getting a mortgage (or any loan for that matter) or interacting with a smart conversational AI-driven chatbot like Alexa in mortgages to get more information on product types or payment holidays. Predictive techniques powered by artificial intelligence (AI) are responsible for such optimizations. While these are some examples of the traditional and mainstream uses of AI in the loan space, this chapter attempts to describe the challenges plaguing the mortgage industry, bolstered heavily by an intermediary-led business model, and some of the latest applications of AI in the mortgage space, especially in mortgage origination, and then explain how AI can further help customers, intermediaries and lenders make more informed decisions to reduce costs, increase revenue and improve overall satisfaction especially when lenders are swamped with phone calls brimming with anxiety. We also attempt to highlight some of the challenges that organisations are facing with specifics on roadblocks to implementation of machine learning in the mortgage industry.

## The Slow and the Furious

We are all aware of the impact of digitisation and other advancements in technology (Briggs 2017). Digitisation has dramatically changed business landscapes across many industries, yielding itself particularly useful in the home buying and owning experience. With a radical shift in favour of digital experiences, consumers are now expecting more from their choicest lenders. Digital transformation is becoming one of the top three strategic priorities for leaders at the helm of these mortgage businesses (Bookallil and Birkby 2017). While more and more lenders were looking to enhance and differentiate their value propositions in the UK with AI applications and support the intermediaries involved in driving businesses adequately prior to the pandemic, digitally enabled mortgage experience seems to be the new trend with distributed teams across geographies committed to serving and supporting their customer base through tumultuous times.

The central premise towards this momentous shift in the UK residential and commercial mortgage industry has been underpinned by the need to act with agility and remain relevant currently in an environment of tepid access to private funding, the heart line for many non-bank entities in UK. This wave of technological innovation is led by AI as start-ups, non-bank lenders, high street lenders and building societies seek ways to automate, de-friction and accelerate each step of the mortgage origination process.

At £65.8 billion, gross mortgage advances in UK commanded a massive mortgage market in 2020 Q1 (Mortgage Lending Statistics 2020). However, the current mortgage origination, which typically characterises the application to the funding journey, is riddled with outdated and cumbersome processes which makes volume handling inefficient and tardy. Moreover, the agonising delays caused by complex paper-driven businesses leave every stakeholder including clients, brokers, surveyors, solicitors and colleagues frustrated with multiple handoffs of paperwork. With a near average of 18–40 days ('How long does it take to get a mortgage?', n.d.), mortgage origination continues to be one of the most wearisome experiences in retail lending. Moreover, customer documents collected at the time of application is a rich source of data, yet lenders continue to struggle with data gathering. There is an overdependence on brokers to ensure reliable information to process and assess applications. Reams of paper need to be then individually analysed and data manually collated, imputed on disparate core-banking platforms leading to the possibilities of human error ('Do we really still have to deal with paper?', 2017). The rise of AI-powered solutions coupled with greater and cleaner data-gathering techniques makes these complications avertable.

In this context, the sudden surge of prominence of challenger entities like Molo and Habito in the UK market can be understood, which are quickly capturing a sizeable market share with their rapid 'mortgage-as-a-service' ('MoloFinance scores £3.7m seed funding to offer a fully digital mortgage', n.d.). Their speed of offering relevant products based on the correct API integrations make them much leaner and efficient in comparison to traditional lenders.

## How Do You Find a Needle in a Haystack?

Many traditional providers continue to search through every nook until they find the needle. With a process, where along with customer experience other stakeholder experience is in question, this approach may seem arduous and counterproductive. Another way is to use a magnet. Smarter fintech lenders are exactly doing that with the use of technology, especially AI, to produce methods to create that magnet leading to their dexterity.

The resurgence of AI comes from a subfield called machine learning. This field involves learning patterns from data without explicitly programming the patterns or rules. An excellent example of automatic learning would be to recognise handwritten digits.

There are two strategies to employ machine learning. The first is via a method called supervised learning where one provides a computer examples along with corresponding solutions and lets the computer figure out the pattern to recognise the different categories or predict a specific outcome. Recognising handwritten digits, a core capability of machine-led extraction, deploys the technique that involves providing the learning algorithm with examples of different handwritten digits and providing the answer it is referring to. Another strategy is to offer an intelligent agent with a problem and let it find the patterns without providing solutions. Clustering data is a problem that can be solved using this strategy. The technical term for this form of automatic learning is called unsupervised learning (Soni 2018).

Imagine if one had all the historical data about the loans over the years. The data would include demographic information, credit scores, as well whether an applicant had defaulted or not. How would you go about using this information to predict the likely outcome of a new application's possible outcome? We can use supervised learning to pre-empt the riskiness of a case and allocate it efficiently. This way lenders can dedicate attention on the specifics of complicated cases and fast-track simple cases with ease, thus saving them valuable time and money.

The AI model would also help save the loan institution money since one can identify very risky applications more assertively and efficiently thereby reducing non-performing assets (NPAs) that will default or get cancelled and accept those that would be profitable. Also, the processing time of a loan application will decrease, leading to higher revenue over time at lower costs.

Another powerful use case of applying machine learning to the loan industry is in the natural language processing and computer vision tasks involved in processing documents. Usually an underwriter needs to spend significant time looking over documents to assess the validity of the papers, scout for relevant data to assess the candidature, and manually impute these onto a loan origination software. One could deploy a state-of-the-art scanning software that employs machine learning capabilities to recognise the characters in a customer/broker-scanned document and analyse it for information that might be useful to the process of underwriting and then directly automate the data-capturing process. With current customer data-privacy challenges impairing the efficacy of implementing open-banking methodologies, extraction technologies can be a powerful compromise ('When open banking and data privacy collide', 2019).

Lenders furthermore risk severe mortgage errors due to lack of adequate AI skills and often draw the ire of regulators. In a recent publication by the Financial Conduct Authority (FCA), there is an added impetus to drive innovation and leverage technology, data and analysis. Sometimes fraud can turn up during the underwriting process, and for the most part, the use of intuition and judgement is used by the underwriter to assess this. The FCA warns against this and encourages the use of intelligent tools to de-risk decision making ('FCA and Bank of England announce proposals for data reforms across the UK financial sector', 2020). Using anomaly detection (a branch of machine learning that seeks to find anomalies/outliers within the data) to detect applications for mortgages/loans that are out of the ordinary can help underwriters efficiently spot fraudulent claims and accelerate relevant actions like financial crime audits earlier in the application cycle saving valuable time.

## Need for Speed: A Case Study

At one of our specialist lending clients in UK, we observed them handling a massive intermediary-sourced business and yet grappling with some of the constraints around scaling up. While there were additional aspirations for leading a direct-to-consumer execution-only business, that share was relatively small, and the priorities were laser-focussed on providing the brokers adequate support for scaling. Also, for a group of environmentally conscious folks, the amount of dependence on paper was undesirable. Coupled with high time to offer, frequent cancellations, revenue leakage, poor colleague-broker-customer experience and high manual errors, the mortgage lending process resulted in an unacceptable net promoter score. Moreover, the pandemic posed a sudden challenge to their modus operandi overnight where colleagues accustomed to co-locating were distributed across homes and shelters. As an outcome of a time-and-motion study that we conducted, we noticed that nearly 40 per cent of the underwriters' time was wasted on non-underwriting related admin work (Digilytics, n.d).

As part of our intervention, the use cases discussed above were all introduced to the mortgage institution to help the team focus on only the complexities of an application that needed experienced eyes and focus on cultivating long-lasting relationships with clients. With intelligence incorporated at the time of application submission, the firm also saved on time and personnel cost with rejection signals identified at the start and lower client cancellations because of long delays.

## The Sane Max Interceptor Model

Many of these applications mentioned have the potential to revolutionise the mortgage industry completely, by speeding up the processing of claims and helping loan institutions reduce costs by decreasing the number of defaults, cancellations using intelligent decision making, as well as improving customer experience. However, for organisations to reap the many benefits of AI, there are a few hurdles that they NEEDS to get through.

There are mainly four significant roadblocks that keep organisations from effectively utilising intelligent agents. They are: integration, explainability, governance and compliance. According to a study on the adoption of machine learning across the UK ('Machine learning in UK financial services' 2019), the constraints to banks and non-bank lending institutions are insufficient data, poor data quality, governance and explainability to name a few.

Integration is the process of effectively assimilating machine learning products and tools into a pre-existing transactional systems. The main problem for organisations here is that the legacy systems involved are often inflexible to such additions or include an abundance of red tape (usually due to security measures). These legacy systems often make it difficult to create seamless user experiences that are generally necessary for adoption. Often such complex systems do not cater to business needs. Consequently, the designed solutions end up wasted and the organisation is unable to reap the rewards. As a viable compromise, many start-ups, including Digilytics AI, have endeavoured to improve the integration problem by creating lightweight modular solutions which have small footprints, and as such do not require a substantial exercise in integration.

Another piece of the puzzle involves the confidence on data models to make it regulation-safe. Explainability strongly connects to governance and compliance. According to the study on the use of machine learning in the UK, 20 per cent of the firms surveyed (in the finance industry) said that explainability was a constraint for their adoption of machine learning ('Machine learning in UK financial services' 2019). From a regulatory perspective, explainability models may additionally help to assess the riskiness of loan books. Moreover, without an ability to articulate clearly and accurately why a model has chosen a particular decision, it becomes hard to decide whether the decision complies. It also becomes difficult to create policies around governance, since the rules these AI agents use are by nature stochastic and not deterministic. There a few ways to mitigate the problem. One can strive to use simpler more well-understood models, such as easily-interpretable linear regression models. However, the main power of AI is its ability to approximate intricate functions and using simpler models may not fit the complex UK mortgage market. A way around this could be to deploy the 'game-theoretic approach of Shapley Values', which attempts to reverse-engineer a working model and assert the importance of individual contributors to determine a target output. Researches have created many methods to make machine learning more explainable (Bracke et al. 2019). Finally, one could also simply educate senior stakeholders in machine learning, making them more aware of how it works as well as the risks involved when deploying such models.

The lack of transparency makes the task of governance a less straightforward endeavour. The job generally includes the process of regulating and controlling the use of machine learning models. By automating lending processes to the degree that they are dehumanised may expose to unwieldy risks and hence explainability is critical to ensure stability. Assessing reasonableness is the subject of a lot of research (Wilkinson and Cevora 2020) and many researchers have developed different measures that assess this quantity. These measures might not solve the problem entirely but will at least create protocols that make errors harder to commit. Retraining models on a predefined schedule lessen the degradation of the explanatory power of the model.

Another profound issue when dealing with these models is the safeguarding of customer data. This issue is not unique to machine learning and is related to the storage of data in general. Still, it is firmly connected, and due consideration must also be taken into account when training these models, all of which requires proper governance.

Assessing compliance consists of many of the same issues as governance. Indeed they are tightly connected as one might imagine. Using the right metrics for different problems and using the test-set evaluation as a benchmark for how well the model is doing is important. For example, if one is performing anomaly detection, it would not be appropriate to use a simple accuracy metric (e.g. counting up the number of correctly detected frauds). For this application, one might want to use metrics such as precision, recall or a weighted sum of those two metrics (e.g. f2-score). The use of such evaluation metrics helps identify the majority non-fraudulent loan applications with a high score. Many issues remain open regarding ensuring the proper use of machine learning to make a critical decision, such as the problem of fairness mentioned earlier. Finally, regulations regarding market abuse and MiFID II (Markets in Financial Instruments Directive), which restrict the use of specific data, limit data availability. According to the study cited in the above learning, a little under 10 per cent of the firms surveyed find these regulations a significant constraint ('Machine learning in UK financial services' 2019). Smart ways of ensuring compliance are needed here.

It is noteworthy that of the firms surveyed on constraints of using machine learning, a little over 20 per cent answered 'general uncertainty'. Machine learning models gain their power from automatic pattern recognition. Instead of the old way of coding rules, the model learns patterns. But the lack of failsafe mechanisms in case the learned heuristics fail makes it a risk to put these models on autopilot. We should think of these models as equivalent to wine, which becomes better with time and, in this case, some trained intervention.

In summary, while the UK AI market is evolutionary and ripe with adequate support from the regulators, machine learning is yet to become mainstream in the dynamic mortgage landscape to enhance customer/user experience. Technology-based lenders who can afford to innovate will have a distinctive competitive advantage to deliver better user experience. In the future, we expect other traditional lenders to emulate fintech players to fully digitise electronic application processes with partially automated underwriting operations. If the greater objective is to transmit some of the central-bank induced liquidity into the market via mortgages, digital transformation will eventually be key in the origination process. However, organisations need to manoeuvre through significant constraints to realise the benefits of AI. These roadblocks include the integration of AI solutions into organisations' legacy systems and dealing with governance, compliance and data privacy. One can mitigate the problem by creating small-footprint solutions, indulging in creative mechanisms to explain models' working and introducing governance regarding code and data quality, peer review, and data privacy. These are just a few of the hacks available today to mitigate these roadblocks. More are yet to come.

## Explanatory Notes

Digilytics RevEl for financial services is a first of its kind, easy to use, least invasive, AI product for revenue growth, built on the most advanced AI technology, making the lending experience seamless. Digilytics RevEl for financial services reduces time to offer for mortgage lenders. The product can be launched from an existing loan origination system and promises to reduce non-value adding manual tasks, augment decision making by providing granular visibility and fast-track underwriting.

## References

Bookallil, Stirling, and Vicky Birkby. 2017. Digital change and mortgage borrowers. Accessed 2 May 2020. https://www.housingnet.co.uk/pdf/digital-change-and-mortgage-borrowers%20(2).pdf.

Bracke, Philippe, Anupam Datta, Carsten Jung and Shayak Sen. 2019. Machine learning explainability in finance: An application to default risk analysis. *SSRN Electronic Journal.* Accessed 4 May 2020. https://doi.org/10.2139/ssrn.3435104.

Briggs, John. 2017. The role of technology in digital transformation. *Ionology.* Accessed 10 May 2020. https://www.ionology.com/the-role-of-technology-in-digital-transformation/.

Digilytics. n.d. Review of time and motion study at a specialist lender. Unpublished.

FCA and Bank of England announce proposals for data reforms across the UK financial sector. 2020. *FCA.* Accessed 4 June 2020. https://www.fca.org.uk/news/press-releases/fca-and-boe-announce-proposals-data-reforms-across-uk-financial-sector.

How long does it take to get a mortgage? n.d. *Bankrate.* Accessed 10 June 2020. https://www.bankrate.com/uk/mortgages/how-long-does-it-take-to-get-a-mortgage/#:~:text=Mortgages%20tend%20to%20take%20around.

Machine learning in UK financial services. 2019. Accessed 12 June 2020. https://www.fca.org.uk/publication/research/research-note-on-machine-learning-in-uk-financial-services.pdf.

MoloFinance scores £3.7M seed funding to offer a fully digital mortgage. n.d. *TechCrunch.* Accessed 14 June 2020. https://techcrunch.com/2018/06/06/molofinance/.

Mortgage lending statistics – March 2020. 2018. *FCA.* Accessed 16 June 2020. https://www.fca.org.uk/data/mortgage-lending-statistics.

Soni, Devin. 2018. Supervised vs. unsupervised learning. *Towards Data Science.* Accessed 18 June 2020. https://towardsdatascience.com/supervised-vs-unsupervised-learning-14f68e32ea8d.

When open banking and data privacy collide. 2019. *American Banker.* Accessed 20 June 2020. https://www.americanbanker.com/opinion/when-open-banking-and-data-privacy-collide.

Why do any of us still have to fill in paper forms to deal with banks and mortgage lenders? 2017. *The Independent.* Accessed 11 May 2020. https://www.independent.co.uk/money/spend-save/paperless-banking-lending-mortgages-online-account-internet-forms-a7969916.html.

Wilkinson, Kate, and George Cevora. 2020. Demonstrating Rosa: The fairness solution for any data analytic pipeline. *Arxiv.org.* Accessed 25 June 2020.https://arxiv.org/abs/2003.00899.

# Chapter 5

# ARTIFICIAL INTELLIGENCE IN GERMANY: STRATEGY AND POLICY— THE IMPACT OF AI ON GERMAN ECONOMY

## Mehrdad S. Sharbaf

## Introduction

Artificial intelligence (AI) is a new digital frontier, and it represents uncharted territory that will be a profound driving force on the global economy, social affairs, and will transform the way we live and work. Over the past decade, AI has matured considerably and, as a fundamental innovation, is becoming the driver of digitalization and autonomous systems in all areas of life. As AI moves from the theoretical concept to the global marketplace, its growth is energized by a great quantity of digitized data and rapidly advancing computational processing power. AI can (1) improve weather forecasting, advanced manufacturing processes, speech recognition, industrial productivity, (2) improve and enhance cybersecurity defenses, (3) boost agricultural productivity, (4) enhance detection of cancer in the medical field, (5) predict an epidemic, and (6) help in development of autonomous vehicles and autonomous weapons systems. For these reasons Germany has initiated a holistic approach to their AI strategy within the European Union. Germany is already extremely well situated in many areas of AI. In the 2019 federal budget, the German Government Federation has taken the first step, allotting a total of €500 million to reinforce the AI strategy for 2019. In the following years, up to and including 2025, the German Government Federation intends to provide around €3 billion for the implementation of the strategy. This chapter seeks to discuss the framework for a holistic strategy and the policy for future development and application of AI in Germany. This chapter also shows that AI holds enormous potential and has a positive impact on German economy due to the technical capabilities of German companies, skilled workers, and a demand in the market for AI services.

Businesses and business processes are continuously evolving due to technological advancement. The need for competitive advantages in businesses has historically been the engine for development of advanced and cost-effective new mechanisms. In this effort, the third industrial revolution emerged in the IT environment, which in turn gave rise to widespread digitalization and moved to the fourth industrial revolution. In Germany, the term "Industry 4.0," has been embraced by the German industry (Hannover fair 2011), which is one of the main indications of this new technological shift and is part of the High-Tech Strategy 2020. In Germany Industry 4.0 was launched by three major German industry associations, BITKOM, ZVEI and VDMA, in 2013, to collaborate their ideas and promote the fourth industrial revolution. These three associations discovered that Industry 4.0 needed to cover social issues and hence decided to surrender leadership to federal government ministries. Research shows that AI offers enormous potential to German economy. A PwC research report forecasts that by 2030, AI alone can increase German gross domestic product (GDP) by 11.3 percent and generate a revenue of €430 billion. As the driving force behind new technological advancements and the fourth industrial revolution, AI is having a profound impact on the world economy, social progress, and people's daily lives, thereby ushering a new era of innovation in our society. In today's society, AI has a clear impact on various industries including manufacturing, cybersecurity, transportation, healthcare, banking, automotive, and many more. Within the past decade, applications of AI in German public administrations have started to emerge. Indeed, AI presents one of the most exciting and promising technologies to support the German government in its e-government transformation process. We observe increasing usage of virtual assistants such as Siri of Apple, Cortana of Microsoft, Alexa of Amazon, and Google Assistant in Germany and in other countries. These conversational agents are based on AI technology, and they are indeed among the most used in AI applications in customer service. To elaborate further about AI, the term artificial intelligence (AI) was initiated at the Dartmouth conference in 1955. It uses a set of computer science and statistical techniques that enables systems to accomplish tasks that normally require human intelligence, such as speech recognition, decision making, and language translation. Machine learning and deep learning are branches of AI that, based on algorithms and powerful data analysis, enable computers to learn and adapt independently. Many of today's AI applications are based on data-driven, machine-learning processes. These methods require large amounts of pre-structured data that are used to teach algorithms. AI systems are viewed primarily as learning systems. Basically machine learning process is a study of algorithms that improve performances of some tasks with experience and optimize a performance criterion using example data or past experience. In the machine learning processes, statistical techniques apply to sample data, and the role of statistical techniques is entrusted with drawing inferences from the sample data. Computer science makes efficient algorithms to solve the optimization problem, and in machine learning processes the role of computer science is to represent and evaluate the model for understanding statistical sample data.

Figure 5.1 represents the machine leaning process with two different data modeling techniques: supervised (inductive) learning wherein training data includes desired outputs; and unsupervised learning wherein training data does not include desired outputs. Figure 5.2 represents the deep learning process. Deep learning algorithms attempt to learn (multiple levels of) representation by using a hierarchy of multiple layers. If you provide the system tons of information, it begins to understand it and respond in useful ways.

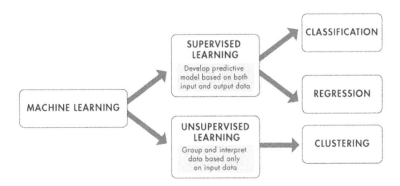

**Figure 5.1** Machine learning process

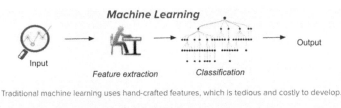

**Figure 5.2** Comparison between machine learning and deep learning

### Research on AI in Germany

German Research Center for Artificial Intelligence (DFKI) was founded in 1988 as a non-profit public private partnership (PPP). With a budget of €45.9 million and 550 employees from 60 countries (2017), it carries out projects in 18 research areas. In order to bring research, development and application of AI in Germany to a global leading stage, an educated and informed society is essential. For this reason, when it comes to AI research, Germany is well positioned with institutions such as the Karlsruhe Institute of Technology, the German Research Center for Artificial Intelligence and the New Cyber Valley research groups, which conduct research in machine learning, robotics, virtual and augmented reality, and computer vision at the Universities of Stuttgart and Tübingen. Germany is at the forefront of AI in Europe, with leaders from various industries working and collaborating alongside top research universities in southwest Germany's Cyber Valley to innovate and develop sophisticated machines with wide capabilities. The German government's initiative is critical to promoting the development of AI, and, among other things, has set up a national research consortium and a Franco-German research and innovation network. These days there are numerous initiatives designed to ensure that AI is developed and used in ways to support humans and the society. For this reason the German government has organized a new program under a broad-based societal dialogue via the Plattform Lernende Systeme. The program consists of two hundred experts from companies and research institutions on this platform. "We must enter into an open dialogue with all segments of society about the potential and risks of AI. This is the only way in which people will come to trust the technology and leverage its opportunities for Germany and Europe", said Karl-Heinz Streibich, the platform's cochair and president of the National Academy of Science and Engineering (Streibich 2019).

## German Strategy and Policy on AI

The German Federal Government's Artificial Intelligence (AI) Strategy was jointly developed and created by the Federal Ministry of Education and Research, the Federal Ministry for Economic Affairs and Energy, and the Federal Ministry of Labor and Social Affairs. The German government's strategy for AI published on November 2018 to bring research, development, and application of AI in Germany to a worldwide leading level. The strategy consists of 12 fields of action-oriented items, and to support these 12 fields, the German government established 14 goals to pursue its national strategy related to AI. The strategy gives great importance to the responsible use of

AI for the benefit and progress of society. In the 2019 federal budget, the federation has taken the first step, allocating a total of €500 million to support the AI strategy for 2019 and the following years. Up to and including 2025, the federation plans to provide around €3 billion for the implementation of the strategy. A brief summary of the AI strategy of the German government is listed below:

1. **Strengthen research in Germany and Europe to be a driver of innovation**

   This is to be accomplished by implementing a strong, dynamic, flexible, broad and interdisciplinary AI ecosystem in Germany that is internationally competitive. Excellent research, to recruit first-class experts and to create an innovation-friendly environment to support the AI strategy.

2. **Innovation competitions and European innovation clusters**

   To create freedom within AI competitions to stimulate disruptive ideas, to find new solutions, applications and business models, to initiate start-ups, to attract talent and to identify trends at an early stage.

3. **Transfer to business, strengthen medium-sized businesses**

   The German government will concentrate on mechanisms that will enable German companies of all sizes, from start-ups, small, and medium size to large corporations, not only to use AI applications but also to develop them and integrate them into their business processes.

4. **Fostering the founding of new businesses and leading them to success**

   To improve access to venture capital as a whole, especially in the growth phase, which is often capital-intensive for AI-based business models. The Ffederal government will create specific incentives for investors and encourage and promote a significantly higher number of spin-offs from research.

5. **World of work and labor market: Shaping structural change**

   The use of AI will fundamentally impact and change the everyday working lives of many people. The Federal government will support all employees in this change with a variety of measures based on a national continuing education strategy.

6. **Strengthening vocational training and attracting skilled labour/experts**

The Federal German government will use all efforts to improve the framework conditions for AI in Germany and will also encourage and support the Federal German states to do so. For this reason the German government needs to promote AI among young people, and to develop new content and ideas for initial, continuing, and further training. Germany also needs to create new chairs at the university level.

7. **Using AI for tasks reserved for the state and administrative workforce**

The Federal government will take a position as a pioneering role model by using AI in its administration and will present faster, better, and more efficient administrative services for the citizens.

8. **Making data available and facilitating its use**

The Federal German government will significantly increase the amount of usable, high-quality data in order to establish Germany as the world's leading AI location without violating personal privacy rights.

9. **Adapting the regulatory framework**

The Federal German government will review the policy and adapt legal frameworks for algorithm- and AI-based decisions, services, and products to make certain effective protection against bias, discrimination, manipulation, or other misuse.

10. **Setting standards**

The Federal German government needs to set up a standard policy for AI. For this reason, the Federal government will work in close contact and in with cooperation with business representatives in the field of AI for standards and standard setting at national, European, and international level through the national standards organizations DIN/DKE (DKE German Commission for Electrical, Electronic & Information Technologies). This is not only about technical issues but also about ethical ones.

11. **National and international networking**

In the near future, cross-sectional technologies such as AI will affect all areas of science, business, administration, and the everyday lives of citizens. Hence, development of AI is global, which is why the government also has to think and act across borders. The Federal government will therefore increasingly expand international cooperation and bilateral and multilateral cooperation in the field of AI.

12. **Engaging in dialogue with society and continuing the development of the framework for policy action**

In order to bring research, development, and application of AI in Germany to a worldwide leading level, an educated and informed society is needed. For that reason, the Federal government will intensify dialogue with society and continue the development of the frame-work for policy action related to education on AI. To support its national strategy the Federal German Government follows 14 goals as follow:

1. Quality plays an important role in AI, and "Artificial Intelligence (AI) made in Germany" is to become a globally recognized seal of quality.
2. Germany should expand its strong position in Industry 4.0 and become a leader in AI applications in this area. The strong German mid-market sector should also benefit from AI applications.
3. Germany is to become an attractive location for the world's best and brightest AI talents
4. The usage of AI in society should focus on the benefits of AI for citizens.
5. To collect data for AI purposes, data is to be used exclusively for the benefit of society, citizens, environment, economy, and the state.
6. With a new infrastructure of internet such as IoT for real-time data transmission, the basis for new AI applications is to be created.
7. Cybersecurity plays an important role in any country, and AI in Germany is to be accompanied by a high level of IT security.
8. Legal framework and ethics are an important part of AI in Germany, and AI research and use should be ethically and legally embedded.
9. Many of today's AI applications are based on data-driven processes. A European response to data-based business models and new ways of data-based value creation is to be found, which corresponds to our economic, value, and social structure.
10. In the global working environment, it should always be about AI for the benefit of all gainfully employed persons.
11. The usage of AI should make living and working areas safer, more efficient, and more sustainable.
12. In German society, AI is intended to promote social participation, freedom of action, and self-determination for citizens.

13. The potential of AI should be used for sustainable development and thus contribute to achieving the sustainability goals of Agenda 2030.
14. For developing AI applications, framework conditions are set, which create and maintain diversity and guarantee the space offered for the development of cultural and media freedom.

On the business front, major automobile companies such as Volkswagen, BMW, and Daimler are investing heavily in modern, AI-controlled factories. They are functioning on solutions for assisted and autonomous driving, intelligent operating systems, entertainment systems, and navigation systems at their German R&D centers. Also, the DFKI Robotics Innovation Center (RIC) is active in a number of robotic application domains, including robotics for inspection and maintenance, space and maritime environments, production, mobility, and healthcare. In the RIC, tests are carried out to maximize the use of collaborative AI robots and link augmented reality technology to AI-based production planning systems..

Germany is also developing as a preferred hub for start-ups focusing on AI and its applications. The most common areas of focus for these AI start-ups are software development, image recognition, customer support, and communication. For example, MonitorFish based in Berlin has developed an approach for intelligent real-time monitoring of aquacultures in fish farming. The Wandelbot based in Dresden start-up offers technology that enables people to programme robots even without expert knowledge. This Merantix startup based in Berlin aims to support companies to convert the results of AI research into practical applications in different industries, namely the automotive and health sectors.

## Conclusion

In the near future, AI will change our global work force and take it to a new horizon compared to the automation and digitalization processes. For this reason, the German government's key approach to AI is to follow a holistic, human-centric, and user-centered approach as they develop AI for the workforce and apply it to good use there. Only if these requirements are met will we be in a position to fully harness the potential for innovation and the productivity gains that AI promises to deliver in Germany.

The German Government's AI Strategy is contributing to the implementation of the current High-Tech Strategy 2025, which focuses on AI as a forward-looking capability for Germany's economy and which defines the transfer of AI into applications as a joint mission with the Federal Germany Government Strategy. Germany is in a good position to become one of the key players in the important discipline of AI.

## Bibliography

Akkaya, Cigdem, and Helmet Krcmar. (2019). Potential use of digital assistants by governments for citizen services: The case of Germany. ACM 2019: Proceedings of the 20th Annual International Conference on Digital Government Research. June 2019. https://doi.org/10.1145/3325112.3325241.

Sonntag, D. (2018). AI in Germany: Well-prepared and eager to do something. *Künstl Intell* 32, 97–99. doi:10.1007/s13218-018-0555-7.

Kim, Gyupan, Lee, Hyong-Kun, Kim, Jonghyuk, and Kwon, Hyuk Ju. (2018). The fourth industrial revolution in major countries and its implications of Korea: U.S., Germany and Japan cases. 23 July. KIEP Research Paper, World Economy Brief 18–20. Available at SSRN: https://ssrn.com/abstract=3304923 or http://dx.doi.org/10.2139/ssrn.3304923.

Harhoff, Dietmar, Heumann, Stefan, Jentzsch, Nicola, and Lorenz, Philippe. (2018). Outline for a German strategy for artificial intelligence. *SSRN Electronic Journal*, https://papers.ssrn.com/sol3/papers.cfm?abstract_id=3222566

Book, Artificial Intelligence. Geneva, Swiss: World Intellectual Property Organization, 2019, https://www.wipo.int/edocs/pubdocs/en/wipo_pub_1055.pdf.

Germany (2018). Artificial Intelligence Strategy. Federal Ministry of Education and Research, the Federal Ministry for Economic Affairs and Energy, and the Federal Ministry of Labour and Social Affairs. https://www.ki-strategie-deutschland.de/home.html?file=files/downloads/Nationale_KI-Strategie_engl.pdf.

Artificial Intelligence: How knowledge is created, transferred, and used trends in China, Europe, and the United States. Annual Report. 2018. https://www.elsevier.com/?a=827872.

Deloitte (2018). Artificial intelligence: Innovation report. https://www2.deloitte.com/content/dam/Deloitte/de/Documents/Innovation/Artificial-Intelligence-Innovation-Report-2018-Deloitte.pdf.

Dickow, M., and Jacob, D. (2018). The global debate on the future of artificial intelligence: The need for international regulation and opportunities for German foreign policy. (SWP Comment, 23/2018). Berlin: Stiftung Wissenschaft und Politik -SWP-Deutsches Institut für Internationale Politik und Sicherheit. https://nbn-resolving.org/urn:nbn:de:0168-ssoar-57759-3.

McKinsey Global Institute. (2017). Artificial intelligence: The next digital frontier? https://www.mckinsey.com/global-themes/artificial-intelligence.

Dopico, M., Gomez, Alberto, Fuente, David, García, N., Rosillo, R., and Puche Regaliza, J. (2016). A vision of Industry 4.0 from an artificial intelligence. International Conference on Artificial Intelligence (IC-AI 2016). https://www.researchgate.net/publication/305073161_A_Vision_of_Industry_40_from_an_Artificial_Intelligence.

Schuessler, M. (2018). Suspending or shaping the AI policy frontier: Has Germany become part of the AI strategy fallacy? Oxford Insights, https://www.oxfordinsights.com/insights/germanyai.

Segal, E. (2021). The Impact of AI in cybersecurity, IEEE Computer Society Publication. https://www.computer.org/publications/tech-news/trends/the-impact-of-ai-on-cybersecurity.

Streibich, Karl-Heinz (2019). Lernende Systeme—Germany's platform for artificial intelligence. Accessed 17 July 2021. https://en.acatech.de/project/learning-systems-the-platform-for-artificial-intelligence/.

# Chapter 6

# JAPAN'S 'ARTIFICIAL-INTELLIGENCE HOSPITAL' PROJECT: CAN IT HELP THE AGEING POPULATION?

## Faith Hatani

## Introduction

As the term artificial intelligence (AI) has become a buzzword in industry and academia in recent years, governments around the world have raced to create national AI strategies. AI can be broadly defined as 'the study of how to make computers do things at which, at the moment, people are better' (Rich et al. 2009, 3). Japan was one of the first countries, alongside Canada, to formulate an AI strategy, publicizing its first in early 2017. This first version of Japan's 'Artificial Intelligence Technology Strategy' prioritized 'health, medical care and welfare', alongside 'productivity' and 'mobility' (Strategic Council for AI Technology, Japan 2017). AI technologies are increasingly penetrating our daily lives, and one of the industries that AI is radically transforming is, indeed, healthcare.

AI, alongside the Internet of Things (IoT) and the Internet of Medical Things, is expected to aid the development of new medicines, reduce diagnostic errors and help doctors more efficiently perform complex surgery with AI-assisted medical robotics (AoMRC 2019). The implementation of AI technologies in healthcare is particularly important in Japan because it is the most rapidly ageing society in the world (IIASA 2018). Japan is now facing serious societal challenges, such as the increasing elderly population and an acute workforce shortage, especially in the healthcare industry. The successful application of AI will enable Japan to sustain its healthcare and improve its medical productivity. In order to achieve these goals, however, effective interactions between the public and private sectors are indispensable. This chapter critically examines Japan's strategy to facilitate such interactions, focusing on its national project to develop so-called 'AI hospitals'.

## Japan's Ageing Society and AI in Healthcare

The development of AI in Japan has largely been a government-led process. The Council for Science, Technology and Innovation (CSTI) of the Japanese government launched the cross-ministerial Strategic Innovation Promotion (SIP) programme in 2013 to stimulate technological innovation in the country. Subsequently, SIP has served as a roadmap for AI development in Japan. Before the promulgation of the 2017 AI technology strategy, the development schemes of technological innovation was designed in two phases. The first phase began in 2014 while the second commenced in 2018. In the first phase, healthcare was not included in SIP's target areas but was kept under a healthcare policy (CSTI 2015). In the second phase, however, health/medical care was integrated into the SIP to create innovative AI hospital systems.

The inclusion of healthcare in SIP reflects a need for fundamental changes to Japan's healthcare. In fact, Japan requires urgent reform of its hospitals and healthcare system as its population has been ageing at an astonishing pace. As of 2018, the proportion of people aged 65 or older accounted for 28 per cent of the total Japanese population (World Bank 2019), giving rise to the label 'super-aged society' (Baba 1993). Japan also has the highest elderly dependency ratio among the OECD's 37 member states; based on current trends, Japan's elderly dependency percentage is projected to increase to 73 per cent in 2050 (OECD 2018). By that time, the country's demographic crunch will have reached its breaking point, which could cause serious social problems. Moreover, Japan's ageing population is not just a social issue but an economic problem too. Since its citizens are provided with well-established universal health and long-term care (LTC) coverage, the increasing elderly population, and thus the rising healthcare and LTC expenditure, is adding to the national debt. Hence, the implementation of AI in the healthcare industry is essential for Japan to optimize its healthcare system and medical practices while maintaining the affordability of healthcare to the population.

### Japan's Ambition for AI Hospitals

In order to tackle its ageing society, the Japanese government launched the AI hospital project in 2018 as part of SIP. By utilizing AI technologies, the project also aims to enhance the competitiveness of Japan's healthcare industry. The AI hospital project consists of the following five sub-themes:

- Sub-theme A: A highly secure medical database and analytical technologies to provide medically useful information.

- Sub-theme B: An AI-assisted automated medical record system and support for mutual communication between medical staff and patients in the process of obtaining informed consent.
- Sub-theme C: AI-assisted, highly sensitive and low-invasive testing of blood and other biological samples to enable the earliest detection of cancer and other serious diseases.
- Sub-theme D: Proof-of-concept study of AI hospital functions in clinical practice settings.
- Sub-theme E: Technical standardization of the AI hospital system, management of intellectual property rights, open and closed innovation strategies, and government–industry–academia collaboration. (CAO 2018, 1–4)

At the outset, the Japanese government made an open call for research and development (R&D) projects under these sub-themes, and eventually, 14 research organizations and groups were selected (Figure 6.1). The selected members include various types of entities, including companies, university hospitals and think tanks. To develop AI hospitals, the Japanese government allocated 3 billion yen to the theme-specific R&D in the 2019 fiscal year alone. Since then, the member organizations have been working on the AI hospital project under respective sub-themes to promote AI technologies and AI-assisted practices.

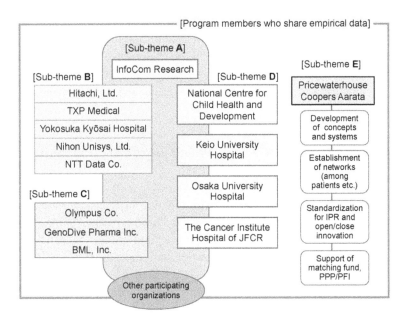

**Figure 6.1** Sub-theme participants of the AI hospital project
*Source*: Adopted from JMA (2019).

In Sub-theme A, InfoCom Research – a Japanese think tank that specializes in the application of information and communications technology (ICT) – has a key role in harnessing project members in the AI hospital project to facilitate research activities. The majority of the R&D projects, especially those in Sub-themes B and C, have a specific partner organization with which joint experiments are conducted. In Sub-theme B, for example, Hitachi, a Japanese electronics conglomerate, develops smart communication technologies to reduce the workload of healthcare employees (Hitachi Co. 2019); since the summer of 2019, Hitachi's communication robots have been installed at the National Centre for Global Health and Medicine, which is part of the Ministry of Health, Labour and Welfare (MHLW). Another example is Olympus, a Japanese optics and imaging company, which has been developing AI-supported endoscopes to detect cancer, in collaboration with another Japanese electronics multinational, NEC (NIBIOHN 2018). In Sub-theme D, four hospitals were selected to establish voice recognition technologies, comprehensive databases and information services for their patients via smartphone apps.

Currently, however, databases and new technologies/practices are being separately developed within each hospital. Moreover, as Figure 6.1 suggests, it is not entirely clear how the outcomes of the sub-theme projects will be linked effectively. Although general knowledge-sharing mechanisms, such as liaison meetings and basic online platforms, have been set up for project members, there is no established channel through which the members will engage with a wider range of stakeholders. This could raise institutional barriers that inhibit interactions across sectors, and it may also discourage foreign entities' involvement in advancing AI in the Japanese market. The following sections will discuss these aspects and potential drawbacks.

## Institutional Obstacles to the Development of AI Hospitals

### Japan's Weak Triple Helix

Since healthcare is a vital and complex function in society, effective cross-sector collaboration is key to the successful implementation of AI. Having recognized this, Japan's SIP emphasizes the importance of collaborative interactions among universities, industries and the government. This tripartite interaction for innovation, which is called a triple helix of innovation (Leydesdorff and Etzkowitz 1998), is a crucial framework upon which to advance AI. However, cross-sectoral interactions for innovation are still underdeveloped in Japan. Most innovation in the country has been carried out by large companies that belong to corporate groups, so-called *keiretsu*, and the role played by universities and public research institutes in innovation has been relatively limited compared to their counterparts in other advanced nations, especially the UK and the United States (OECD 2018). Japanese universities and public research institutes tend to be strongly oriented towards basic research, and they are not active enough in product development for the commercial or practical use of new technologies (Araiso 2014).

Moreover, although Japan has large and internationally competitive firms in the manufacturing sector, notably in the automotive industry, it does not have strong business actors that can take a leadership role in the healthcare industry. For instance, in terms of R&D sector specialization, more than 31 per cent of Japan's industrial R&D was concentrated in the automotive industry, and the healthcare industry had just 12.5 per cent in 2019, whereas in the EU and the United States in the same year, the ratios of R&D investments in healthcare industries were 19.2 per cent and 24.5 per cent respectively (European Commission/Joint Research Centre 2020). To strengthen university–industry–government collaboration, a series of policy reforms and incentives have been implemented in the past few decades, and some studies have recognized the recent improvement in Japan's triple helix (e.g. Leydesdorff and Sun 2009; Rieu 2014). Nonetheless, policy reforms and incentives tend to be company-oriented (OECD 2018), and the pace of institutional change in Japan is, in general, notoriously slow (Hatani 2020). To encourage cross-sector collaboration for healthcare AI and to avoid the fragmentation of different actors' efforts, a more effective coordination mechanism is required.

### Issues with the National Innovation System

Japan's relatively weak triple helix is closely associated with issues with its national innovation system. A national innovation system refers to a network of various institutions that contribute to the advancement and diffusion of new technologies in a country (Metcalfe 1995; Nelson 1993). It consists of regulations, financial mechanisms and other socioeconomic factors in a given country. During the 1980s, Japan's innovation system was regarded as high-performing, based on tightly knit relationships among the country's leading companies (Mowery and Rosenberg 1993). Since the onset of the economic recession in the 1990s, however, its competitive edge has been eroded.

Several institutional factors have contributed to slowing the development of AI in Japan. First, Japan has a very limited amount of venture capital investments; the volume of venture capital in Japan is only 10 per cent of that in the United States (Araiso 2014). This business environment makes entrepreneurship in the high-tech sector more difficult. Second, the ageing population has also contributed to the decline of R&D investment because the domestic savings of the younger generation, which are an important source of capital growth, are constantly declining (Goto 2000). Another issue pertains to Japan's ethnocentric approach to innovation. An official document prepared by the Japanese government explicitly states that the intention is to develop AI hospitals and related medical AI platforms via 'All Japan'; that is, through collective efforts made by Japanese firms and domestic research institutes, rather than by collaborating with foreign entities (CAO 2018). Considering the key characteristics of AI, such as the use of big data and new technologies that are likely to shape new international standards in the near future, Japan's nationalistic mindset would be detrimental because it will limit effective knowledge sharing in an international sphere. Given these factors, it is not surprising that Japan is now lagging behind not only major advanced nations but also China in terms of AI readiness (Oxford Insights 2019). Unless Japan changes its rules and norms concerning new technologies, it is questionable whether its AI hospitals will succeed in the digital age.

### *Lagging Digital Transformation*

Concerning the use of ICT in the workplace, Japan's digitalization is lagging behind other G7 nations (except Italy) and Nordic countries (OECD 2019). This factor, together with the rigid regulations in Japan, has significantly slowed the effective interface between medical practices and digital technologies. One such example that has suffered from sluggish development is online medical consultation and diagnosis. Although there had been a call for the deregulation of this type of online service to increase the access to medical examinations, the government – in this case, the MHLW as the responsible body – persistently upheld restrictions on online medical services. In the spring of 2020, the regulation was finally relaxed amid the COVID-19 pandemic, but it was only a temporary easing of the rules as a countermeasure against the rise of coronavirus infections. Access to online diagnosis remains largely limited because very few medical institutes have suitable facilities to adequately provide an online diagnosis (Nihon Keizai Shimbun 2020).

Given that well-functioning online medical services are still limited in Japan, and that elderly people tend to live in rural areas and/or have limited physical mobility, the AI project is now paying closer attention to mobility-as-a-service (MaaS) through the use of autonomous vehicles (AVs). Indeed, mobility is one of the areas that has been prioritized in Japan's AI strategy, and the Japanese automotive industry has a competitive advantage. If MaaS, backed by safer and more efficient AVs, is utilized in healthcare, it will make it easier for the elderly or those with limited mobility to travel to their medical appointments (KPMG International 2019). If necessary, this could also enable patients to visit AI hospitals, which are mainly located in large cities. In addition, as part of the recent 'medical AI platform' vision in the AI hospital project (JMA 2020), there has been a new healthcare mobility experiment to support the elderly and those who have very limited mobility. Rather than making patients visit a hospital, an AV equipped with essential devices, such as a blood pressure monitor, glucose meter and pulse oximeter, as well as a nurse, will come to each patient's doorstep (Iwasada 2020). In a way, this is a form of home delivery of an online health check and diagnosis for those whose mobility is impeded as well as for those who have difficulty accessing the internet to make a video call for online diagnosis. Patients can have a full check-up with a nurse's help on a healthcare mobility AV (Iwasada 2020). However, when, and the extent to which this healthcare mobility will be put into practice depends largely on how effectively and swiftly regulations can adapt to the new methods.

## Concluding Remarks

Over the past several decades, Japan has developed one of the most well-established universal healthcare systems in the world. However, due to internal economic and demographic changes, Japanese healthcare is at a crossroads. On the surface, the large investment in AI hospitals appears to represent a reasonable approach by the government. Since its efforts to apply AI technologies to the healthcare industry are still at an early stage, as is AI itself, it is premature to make a judgment on Japan's AI hospital project at the present time. Nonetheless, the AI project requires a more effective coordination mechanism and a sensible international perspective to address key issues in the country. Potentially a controversial issue in this regard is the Japanese government's ultimate goal. According to the government plan of 2018, it aims to commercialize AI hospitals as a new business model in the healthcare industry and to tap into the healthcare markets abroad (CAO 2018). This raises concerns that the AI hospital project is not prioritizing the country's ageing population sufficiently. The real challenge to Japan's AI in the healthcare industry relates not solely to technology but more to the setting of goals, and the coordination mechanism required to achieve these goals.

All in all, the Japanese government needs to understand that technological upgrading of the healthcare industry requires significant investment, not just in new technologies but ultimately in human capital. Medical professionals need to ensure that their voices are heard, and companies should commit themselves more to contribute to tackling societal challenges with their resources and technologies in order to guide, rather than simply being guided by, the government agenda. More human-centred and inclusive approaches, while recognizing elderly people as key members of society, should be at the centre of healthcare AI. Public and private stakeholders should aim towards this goal to benefit society through AI.

## References

Academy of Medical Royal Colleges (AoMRC). 2019. *Artificial Intelligence in Healthcare*. London: AoMRC.

Araiso, Tsunehisaa. 2014. The structure and function of industry-academia-government cooperation system in USA and Europe. *Sangaku Renkei Gaku*, 10(1): 1–12.

Baba, Shigeaki. 1993. The super-aged society. *World Health*, 46(3): 9–11.

Cabinet Office (CAO), Japan. 2018. 戦略的イノベーション創造プログラム (SIP): AI（人工知能）ホスピタルによる高度診断・治療システム 研究開発計画 [Strategic Innovation Promotion (SIP) program: Advanced diagnosis and treatment system by AI]. Accessed 26 December 2019. https://www8.cao.go.jp/cstp/gaiyo/sip/iinkai2/aihospital.html.

Council for Science, Technology and Innovation (CSTI). 2015. Science and technology basic plan. Accessed 26 December 2019. https://www8.cao.go.jp/cstp/english/panhu/2_p3-5.pdf.

European Commission/Joint Research Centre. 2020. *The 2020 EU Industrial R&D Investment Scoreboard*. Luxembourg: European Union.

Goto, Akira. 2000. Japan's national innovation system: Current status and problems. *Oxford Review of Economic Policy*, 16(2): 103–13.

Hatani, Faith. 2020. Artificial intelligence in Japan: Policy, prospects and obstacles in the automotive industry. In Anshuman Khare, Hiroki Ishikura, and William Baber (eds), *Transforming Japanese Business: Rising to the Digital Challenge*, pp. 211–26. Singapore: Springer.

Hitachi Co. 2019. News release. 17 September 2019. https://www.hitachi.co.jp/New/cnews/month/2019/09/0917.html.

International Institute for Applied System Analysis (IIASA). 2018. *Aging Demographic Data Sheet 2018*. Laxenburg, Austria: IIASA.

Iwasada, R. 2020. '医療MaaSが官民協働体制で走り出す'. Accessed 22 December 2020. https://sip-cafe.media/column/3528/.

Japan Medical Association (JMA). 2019. '戦略的イノベーション創造プログラム (SIP) AI ホスピタルによる高度診断・治療システム成果発表シンポジウム2019開催について'. Accessed 27 December 2019. http://dl.med.or.jp/dl-med/teireikaiken/20191009_2.pdf.

———. 2020. '医療AIプラットフォーム構想を発表'. Accessed 24 December 2020. http://www.med.or.jp/nichiionline/article/009398.html.

KPMG International. 2019. 2019 autonomous vehicles readiness index: Assessing countries' preparedness for autonomous vehicles. Accessed 22 December 2020. https://assets.kpmg/content/dam/kpmg/xx/pdf/2019/02/2019-autonomous-vehicles-readiness-index.pdf.

Leydesdorff, Loet, and Henry Etzkowitz. 1998. The triple helix as a model for innovation studies. *Science and Public Policy*, 25(3): 195–203.

Leydesdorff, Loet, and Yuan Sun. 2009. National and international dimensions of the triple helix in Japan: University–industry–government versus international coauthorship relations. *Journal of the American Society for Information Science and Technology*, 60(4): 778–88.

Metcalfe, John S. 1995. The economic foundations of technology policy: equilibrium and evolutionary perspectives. In Paul Stoneman (ed.), *Handbook of the Economics of Innovation and Technological Change*, pp. 409–512. Oxford: Blackwell.

Mowery, David C., and Nathan Rosenberg. 1993. The U.S. national innovation system. In Richard Nelson (ed.), *National Innovation Systems: A Comparative Analysis*, pp. 29–75. Oxford: Oxford University Press.

National Institutes of Biomedical Innovation, Health and Nutrition (NIBIOHN). 2018. Cross-ministerial strategic innovation promotion program: Advanced diagnosis and treatment systems through AI hospitals. Accessed 30 January 2020. https://www.nibiohn.go.jp/nibio/part/promote/sip/saitaku.html.

Nelson, Richard R. ed. 1993. *National Innovation Systems. A Comparative Analysis*. Oxford: Oxford University Press.

Nihon Keizai Shimbun. 2020. オンライン診療、初診も13日に解禁、対応機関はわずか. 13 April . https://www.nikkei.com/article/DGXMZO57968210S0A410C2000000/.

OECD. 2018. *Japan: Promoting Inclusive Growth for an Ageing Society*. Paris: OECD. https://www.oecd.org/about/secretary-general/BPS-Japan-EN-April-2018.pdf.

———. 2019. *OECD Skills Outlook 2019: Thriving in a Digital World*. Paris: OECD. https://doi.org/10.1787/df80bc12-en.

Oxford Insights. 2019. Government artificial intelligence readiness index 2019. Accessed 20 December 2019. https://www.oxfordinsights.com/ai-readiness2019.

Rich, Elaine, Kevin Knight  and Shivashankar B. Nair. 2009. *Artificial Intelligence* (3rd edition). New Delhi: Tata McGraw-Hill.

Rieu, Alain-Marc. 2014. Innovation today: The triple helix and research diversity. *Triple Helix*, 1(8), Art. 8.

Strategic Council for AI Technology, Japan. 2017. Artificial Intelligence Technology Strategy (Report of Strategic Council for AI Technology). Accessed 5 May 2019. https://www.nedo.go.jp/content/100865202.pdf.

World Bank. 2019. Population ages 65 and above (% of total population). Accessed 21 April 2019. https://data.worldbank.org/indicator/SP.POP.65UP.TO.ZS.

# Chapter 7

# ARTIFICIAL INTELLIGENCE IN THE MIDDLE EAST EUROPEAN COUNTRIES

Andrea Bencsik

## Introduction

For the term 'artificial intelligence (AI)' Google searched 797 million results in 0.49 seconds. There were 2,590,000 hits in 0.14 seconds in the 'Scientific paper' category. The increases in scientific publications can be seen in Figure 7.1. The numbers prove the popularity of the topic.

Issues related to AI are addressed at different levels, but with many different approaches. Popularity of AI is not accidental as it is embedded in our daily lives and shapes our thinking and decisions in private and at work. But it poses a serious challenge to an organization's management systems as it is the driving force behind the Fourth Industrial Revolution (Brynjolfsson et al., 2018). International Data Corporation (IDC 2019) analyses that the global value of developments can reach $90 billion by 2023 (Chernov and Chernova 2019).

The contents of publications, studies, blogs and web pages about AI are almost untraceable and the possibilities of understanding and incorporating into an organization's everyday life depend on several factors. The most important of these is *knowledge*, coupled with trust and/or mistrust in technology and its safety. Another important factor is *technical readiness* (development), which determines the integration of AI into everyday practice in a broad range/gamut. The third, also influencing the former two, is *financial conditions*. Other factors can be listed, but the above are closely related, and they distinguish the situation of the countries presented in this study fundamentally from the practices of Western European, American and Asian countries. In the following, the study describes the situation and practice of the group formed in the heart of Central and Eastern Europe, the Visegrad Four.

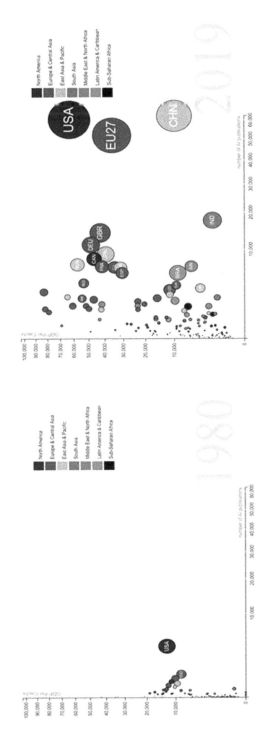

**Figure 7.1** AI publications versus GDP per capita by countries, regions
*Source*: www.oecd.ai.

## AI and the Visegrad Four

Within the European Union (EU), the Visegrad Group (V4) is a regional organisation of four Central European member states – the Czech Republic, Poland, Hungary and Slovakia. Their aim is to jointly represent the economic, diplomatic and political interests of these countries. The V4 was founded in Visegrad (Hungary) in 1991 to promote the development of the region. In 2004, they all joined the EU. These four countries account for more than a tenth of the EU's territory and population, contributing almost 6 per cent of the EU's economic performance in terms of GDP, around 8 per cent of car production, and almost 20 per cent of major crops. These countries also joined forces to develop Industry 4.0, digitisation and AI through economic cooperation. Regional cooperation enables national economies to develop their digital economy and compete in the international market, with a common goal and a unified ideology (Visegrad Group 2020).

The automation potential of the V4s is equal to the world average and higher than the EU average of 44 per cent. The main reason for the difference is the different sectoral composition of the economies. The share of industrial sectors that can be well automated (mostly manufacturing, trade, transportation) is between 31–39 per cent, which is significantly higher than the EU average of 25 per cent. At the same time, public services (e.g. education, health care, social services), expert and communication activities, architecture, and so on, which are less likely to be automated, play a smaller role in the economy of the V4s than in the EU. Overall, approximately 60 per cent of the workforce can be involved in the automation process. There is a growing demand for professionals who design and operate automated technologies.

The V4 countries have several building blocks that are necessary for the efficient integration of automation, especially in the fields of manufacturing and info-communications. They have particularly good results in terms of the use of communication infrastructure, human capital, and the internet. The development of workforce skills (software development, management of automation technologies, etc.) needs to be strengthened (Fine et al., 2018).

V4s are not really active yet, hence the demand for AI experts is low. Professionals active in the field seek jobs in other countries (brain drain also is a problem in European countries). In line with the EU strategy, the recent memorandum of cooperation signed by digital associations and companies of the V4 countries calls for legal and public administrative regulation to support the development of digital economies. According to the signatories, innovative public administration and economic development are a priority if they want to strengthen their position in Central and Eastern Europe. Their aim is to establish research and development centres, as these provide the basis for the emergence of innovative ideas that can later lead to commercial success. The cooperation will also influence cybersecurity, 5G development, Internet of Things (IoT), AI and digital competence education (digitalv4.eu 2019). The V4s believe that they can also send a positive message at the European level about the social and economic aspects of AI. However, the current situation (despite all provincial successes) is unbalanced. Inhabitants, especially in Hungary, have negative opinions about automation, including robots and AI.

## General Knowledge of AI

Due to the popularity of AI, the term frequently appears in conversations, but even among professionals in the region, it is debated whether the essence of the term is well understood, or if AI is just used as a synonym for mechanisation and automation. Where does AI begin, what belongs to it, and what is simply a 'smart' solution? It is also important to clarify this term for lay people as this understanding can raise confidence in the use of advanced technologies and software.

Digitisation and computing capacities are growing steadily in the region, and the almost limitless databases available provide tremendous opportunities. The development may be interpreted as a result of the data accumulated over years expanded from time to time. However, it was possible to convert this data only in the past few years. Currently, hardware (computing) capacity is what hinders more dynamic development. The data is available, but there is currently no suitable computer capable of handling and processing the entire data set. For the moment, we only process the information that is specific to a particular field. It is generally known that AI makes people's lives easier, and the dangers are also known and can be managed with proper control (Monitoring Progress 2019).

## Factors Influencing the Use of AI

### Knowledge

In 2018, EU member states signed a memorandum of cooperation on AI and the strengthening of Europe's technological and industrial capacities (European Comission 2019b). In the cooperation, the V4s addressed the importance of education and research and development. These areas are particularly important for Slovakia. Its economy is highly industry-specific, and the four car companies Volkswagen, Kia, PSA (Peugeot Citroen's) and Jaguar, and their supplier companies provide a significant proportion of jobs. However, Slovakia is unprepared for automation. An OECD survey (2018) shows that one-fourth of the Slovak population is computer illiterate, and there is a significant deficit of employees trained in info-communications. If Slovakia wants to keep up, it will have to start by transforming the current school system. To do so, a larger share of GDP must be invested in research and development projects. The current value is below 1 per cent, whereas the OECD average is 2.3 per cent.

A PwC study (2019) estimated the possible future outcome in Hungary. By 2030, AI is expected to have significant presence in manufacturing, transportation and construction businesses. Currently, Hungarian companies adhere to traditional methods and slowly adopt and incorporate necessary knowledge into lines of businesses.

### Technical Readiness

Artificial intelligence accelerates economic growth and productivity. For this theoretical possibility to materialise, numerous tech-oriented companies need to be established, with a proper support for their growth. It is necessary for technology to spread, to penetrate economic sectors, and thus increase their productivity. All this means significant investments, company re-organisation and work organisation tasks.

The information and communications technology (ICT) sector, as a generator of new technologies, greatly contributes to efficiency. Its share in the Czech Republic is 5.2 per cent, slightly above the EU average (5.0 per cent), and above the other V4 countries. The digital intensity indicator (value 1–12) introduced by Eurostat expresses the methods of using business information and communication technologies in the business sector. Despite the above, this indicator shows that, in the Czech Republic, more than 80 per cent companies belong to the very low or low categories (Eurostat 2020a).

### Financial Conditions

The V4 is one of the most dynamically developing group of countries in the EU (Gal 2018), but its per capita GDP was well below the EU average in 2019 (Eurostat 2020b). Despite a growing trend in GDP functions, V4 members have not been able to catch up.

Since V4 members have a significantly lower GDP per capita than the EU average, they are less able to contribute to the EU's technological developments. Within the V4, the Czech Republic leads in GDP per capita, with the largest contribution expected of the four members. This means it mostly applies technological innovations instead of creation, so its innovation footprint is smaller. Compared to the EU, its innovative capacity is between

50 and 90 per cent. All V4 countries face similar difficulties – financing their innovation processes is problematic and the number of intellectual assets, that is, patents and trademarks, is low (European Commission 2019a).

## AI Strategies of the V4s

The named influencing factors and development possibilities have been integrated into the strategy of the V4s. The document 'National Artificial Intelligence Strategy of the Czech Republic' (2019) includes the importance of education – training professionals who have complex skills, are multidisciplinary, are IT-minded and are able to fill high value-added positions. As for financing, the strategy highlighted AI-related projects and various grants. As for laws, the elimination of specific legislative barriers, the implementation of public consultation and the preparation of risk analysis played a role (Ministry of Industry and Trade of the Czech Republic, 2019).

The draft version of the Polish AI strategy was completed in August 2019 (European Commission 2019d). Its main goal is to support economic growth and innovation in the knowledge-based society through AI-related science and research. The pillars of the document are the reform of education, support of companies dealing with AI, strengthening of cooperation and digital infrastructure improvement.

Hungary issued its AI-related action plan in October 2019. The document focussed on technological developments, acquisition of competencies to operate them, establishment of a legal background and infrastructure strengthening (European Commission 2019b).

Slovakia outlined its AI-related future plans in the 'Action Plan for the Digital Transformation of Slovakia for 2019–2022' document. The program includes concrete steps to help the establishment of a sustainable, human-centric and trustworthy AI ecosystem (European Commission 2020).

The four countries, although able to engage in R&D activities, including AI developments, are followers rather than innovators. The spread of AI-related activities is mainly expected in the Czech Republic.

## Expected Effects of AI

The biggest issue related to the widespread use of AI is related to human resource management. Workplaces in Slovakia, the citadel of care industry, are most threatened by automation and its consequences (Roy 2020). The OECD forecasts that 34 per cent of the jobs in the country are at risk. In the Czech Republic some professions will cease or their performance will change within 10 to 20 years (MPSV 2016). Fully automated jobs will decline over the next decade. This category includes drivers, packers, power plant operators and postal carriers. The proportion of these jobs is 69 per cent in the Czech Republic (Lordan 2018).

According to a PwC study (2019), the most influential disruptive technological solutions – automation, machine learning and AI – will significantly affect Hungarian employees over the next years. Hungary is basically an industry-focussed economy and hence manufacturing, transportation and construction will be dramatically affected by the spread of AI (OECD 2018). Two-thirds of the jobs belong to these branches. The effects of technological changes will be experienced in the labour market primarily from the 2030s. Estimations predict that AI will have impact on more than 900,000 jobs over the next 15 years. Based on Hungary's economic structure, it can be concluded that the automation of manual, precision-requiring, monotonous tasks can cause the largest rate of change in the labour market (PwC 2019).

## Innovative Businesses in the Light of AI

The Slovak company MultiplexDX is one of the most innovative biotechnological corporations in the market for personalised molecular diagnostics. Its staff come from prestigious institutions such as the National Cancer Institute, Rockefeller University, Albert Einstein University, Queens University (Canada) and the Max Delbrück Center for Molecular Medicine (Germany) (MultiplexDX 2020).

In 2006, the Hungarian company NNG redrew the world of navigation software. NNG's first product, iGO My way, introduced at the CeBIT fair in Hanover, Germany, in 2006, fit on a gigabyte memory card, while competitors needed a DVD (NNG 2020a). With this, they gained world fame, and today they work with partners such as Volkswagen, Nissan and Samsung (NNG 2020b).

The number of users of the innovative solutions of Prezi, an online presentation company, founded in 2009, is ten times more than the population of Hungary. It expanded its headquarters in Budapest with another one in San Francisco, further increasing its global operations (Prezi 2020).

Launched in 2011, the Polish company Zortrax specialises in 3D printing in the global market for desktop printers. Their products primarily target companies but are also sold to individuals in 90 countries (Zortrax 2020). Another Polish company Neoteric specialises in intelligent systems in machine learning, supporting companies with successful software and product development and the use of AI (Neoteric 2020).

In the Czech Republic, a conference and event application, ImpromptMe (ImpromtMe 2020), was created. The company's basic values are simplicity, transparency and fairness, which are indispensable conditions for users. The application's customer base is the world market.

A drawback of the V4 cooperation is that the four countries do not form a market. They have four different currencies, regulations and languages. Their sizes are small and so are their domestic markets. The exception is Poland, which is larger than the total area of the other three members. Thus, for Polish companies, the domestic market provides a sufficient customer base and hence a lesser incentive for international presence.

The fastest-growing tech company in Central Europe is the Czech Prusa Research s.r.o., which develops and sells 3D printers. The company, founded in 2009, had a growth rate of 17,118 per cent between 2014 and 2017 (Prusa3d 2020). A Deloitte study shows that most of the fast-growing tech companies, numbering seventeen, were located in Poland. In comparison, Czech Republic had seven, Slovakia had three and Hungary had two (Deloitte 2018).

## Future in the Focus

There are four areas to work on: open but regulated access to data; retaining talented professionals and training new ones; creating efficiently operable huge computing power and capacity; finally, generating the right algorithms and understanding how they work. Properly managed AI can bring double-digit growth in GDP that no one would want to miss. AI and the devices it controls make anything attackable. Tactical tools such as warships or an aircraft fleet are becoming less and less relevant. Meanwhile, cyber warfare makes it possible not to defeat an opponent on the battlefield but to cause serious problems in the 'hinterland', rendering important infrastructures inoperable or causing social insecurity and confusion.

Finally, the following is a key message summed up in five thoughts:

- The issue of AI is urgent and needs to be addressed at the European level and together
- Good AI is based on the right quality and quantity data and its meaningful processing
- AI will simultaneously create and eliminate jobs, which must be monitored continuously and intervened in time if necessary
- To be prepared for the future, we need more scenarios and more contingencies ready with an action plan,
- We need to act together to put AI at the service of Europe, so the best experts must be kept in Europe.

## Acknowledgement

This work was supported by the TKP2020-NKA-10 project financed under the 2020-4.1.1-TKP2020 Thematic Excellence Programme by the National Research, Development and Innovation Fund of Hungary.

## References

Brynjolfsson, Erik, Daniel, Rock, and Chad, Syverson. (2018). Artificial intelligence and the modern productivity paradox: A clash of expectations and statistics. In Ajay K. Agrawal, Joshua S. Gans and Avi Goldfarb (eds), *The Economics of Artificial Intelligence: An Agenda*, pp. 23–57. Cambridge: National Bureau of Economic Research.

Chernov, Alexey, and Victoria, A. Chernova. (2019). Artificial intelligence in management: Challenges and opportunities. In K. Hammes, M. Machrafi, and A. Samodol (eds), Book of Proceedings, 38th International Scientific Conference on Economic and Social Development 21–22. March 2019. 133–40. Marocco: Rabat.

Deloitte. (2018). Deloitte Technology, Fast 50 Central Europe 2018, powerful connections. https://www2.deloitte.com/content/dam/Deloitte/ce/Documents/about-deloitte/ce-technology-fast-50-2018-report.pdf.

European Commission. (2019a). Communication artificial intelligence, https://ec.europa.eu/digital-single-market/en/news/communication-artificial-intelligence-europe.

———. (2019c). National strategies on artificial intelligence: A European perspective in 2019. Country report – Hungary. https://ec.europa.eu/knowledge4policy/sites/know4pol/files/hungary-ai-strategy-report.pdf.

———. (2019b). National strategies on artificial intelligence: A European perspective in 2019. Country report – Poland. https://ec.europa.eu/knowledge4policy/sites/know4pol/files/poland-ai-strategy-report.pdf.

———. (2020). National strategies on artificial intelligence: A European perspective in 2019. Country report – Slovakia. https://ec.europa.eu/knowledge4policy/sites/know4pol/files/slovakia-ai-strategy-report.pdf.

Eurostat. (2020a). Employed ICT specialists – total. https://appsso.eurostat.ec.europa.eu/nui/show.do?dataset=isoc_sks_itspt&lang=en.

———. (2020b). Real GDP per capita. https://ec.europa.eu/eurostat/databrowser/view/sdg_08_10/default/table?lang=en.

Fine, David, Havas, Andras, Hieronimus, Solveigh, Janoskuti, Levente, Kadocsa, Andras, and Puskas, Peter. (2018). Átalakuló munkahelyek: az automatizálás hatása Magyarországon. [Changed workplaces: The effects of automation in Hungary]. *McKinsey and Company*. https://www.mckinsey.com/~/media/McKinsey/Locations/Europe%20and%20Middle%20East/Hungary/Our%20Insights/Transforming%20our%20jobs%20automation%20in%20Hungary/Automation-report-on-Hungary-HU-May24.ashx.

Gal, Zsolt. (2018). A visegrádi négyek országai főbb regionális gazdasági jellemzői. *Polgári Szemle*, 14(4–6) 301–10. https://doi.org10.24307/psz.2018.1222.

IDC. (2019). Worldwide artificial intelligence spending guide. https://www.idc.com/getdoc.jsp?containerId=IDC_P33198.

ImpromptMe. (2020). About. https://impromptme.com/Company/About.

Letter of intent by the Visegrad Four's innovation leaders regarding a common policy towards development of the digital sector and advanced technologies. (2019). https:// digitalv4.eu/wp-content/uploads/2020/04/Letter-of-intent_V4.pdf.

Lordan G. (2018). *Robots at Work, 2018*. Luxembourg: Publications Office of the European Union. https://ec.europa.eu/social/main.jsp?catId=738&langId=%20 en&pubId=8104&further Pubs=yes ISBN: 978-92-79-80236-2.

Ministry of Industry and Trade of the Czech Republic. (2019). National Artificial Intelligence Strategy of the Czech Republic. https://www.mpo.cz/assets/en/guide-post/for-the-media/press-releases/2019/5/NAIS_eng_web.pdf.

Monitoring Progress in National Initiatives on Digitising Industry. (2019). https:// ec.europa.eu/information_society/newsroom/image/document/2019-32/country_ report_-_hungary_-_final_2019_0D30BE02-9661-9403-6F972D2CCBB689B0_ 61210.pdf.

MPSV. (2016). Iniciativa prace 4.0. https://portal.mpsv.cz/sz/politikazamest/prace_4_0/ studie_iniciativa_prace_4.0.pdf.

MultiplexDX. (2020). Company overview. https://www.multiplexdx.com/multiplexdx# company-overview.

National Artificial Intelligence Strategy of the Czech Republic. (2019). https://www.mpo. cz/assets/en/guidepost/for-the-media/press-releases/2019/5/NAIS_eng_web.pdf.

Neoteric. (2020). https://neoteric.eu/.

NNG. (2020a). Partnereink. https://www.nng.com/partnereink/?lang=hu.

———. (2020b). Történetünk. https://www.nng.com/tortenetunk/?lang=hu.

OECD. (2018). Job creation and local economic development: Preparing for the future of work. https://www.oecd-ilibrary.org/docserver/9789264305342-en.pdf?expires=158 8751825&id=id&accname=guest&checksum=2E2129EFE72FCD29F2CA0FD36C5 02FF0.

OECD.AI. (2020). Visualisations powered by JSI using data from MAG. www.oecd.ai.

Prezi. (2020). About. https://prezi.com/about/?click_source=logged_element&page_ location=footer&element_text=about.

Prusa3d. (2020). About us. https://www.prusa3d.com/about-us/.

PwC. (2019). How will AI impact the Hungarian labour market? https://www.pwc.com/ hu/en/publications/assets/How-will-AI-impact-the-Hungarian-labour-market.pdf.

Roy, Vincent. (2020). *AI Watch – National Strategies on Artificial Intelligence: A European Perspective in 2019*. Luxembourg: Publications Office of the European Union.

Visegrad Group. (2020). http://www.visegradgroup.eu/hu.

Zortrax. (2020). https://zortrax.com/.

# Chapter 8

# A MILLION PRODUCTS FOR A BILLION PEOPLE: ARTIFICIAL INTELLIGENCE IN CONSUMER INDUSTRIES IN INDIA

## Arindom Basu, Rohit Sehgal and Akul Jain

India spans 3.3 million kilometres spread over 7,900 towns and around 600,000 villages. It has approximately 10 million retailers. The fast moving sector, which, along with automobile, consumer durables and pharmaceuticals, makes up the majority of the consumer industries (CI) sector, retails products from around 21,000 manufacturers producing a quarter of a million stock keeping units (SKUs) (Nielsen 2016). Add the other sectors, and the CI sector in India sells a million products to a billion Indians. Imagine doing that only with human intelligence.

The path to achieve stability for artificial intelligence (AI)-based implementation in the CI sector is nascent but the potential is becoming increasingly clear. The adoption of AI-based solutions in India has seen an upward trend in the past few years. Over the past few years, it has been observed that high- and mid-cap CI companies have benefitted from AI in their various practice lines. AI has delivered excellent results in terms of increased revenues, improved productivity and increased effectiveness of their promotional expenditures. Companies have seen tremendous changes in their transactional, distribution and marketing-based processes, thereby improving both top-line and bottom-line growth. The reason behind this key success is the ability of these organizations to combine AI-based technology with the human-in-the-loop to deliver efficient business outcomes at scale.

Having operated in the market for over two years, Digilytics AI, a category leader of easy-to-use SaaS AI products, finds that players in the consumer industry are extremely receptive to the use of AI and analytics to gain first-mover advantage. However, only a selected few companies understand the real benefits of AI and how to apply it. Despite a huge growth in the technology infrastructure in these companies, most continue to struggle with basic data quality issues. However, there is a consensus among business heads that there lies a huge potential in using AI and in all the major business functions within the company. With this positivity in the business sphere, companies have initiated the roll out of AI-based capabilities with the right steps in mind. Given the experience, Digilytics has been consistent in following a structured methodology to harmonize data efficiently, operationalize AI and analytics and reinforce an analytics mindset so that it can react to insights faster and accelerate the pace of business.

Almost every business function team presents within a company is capable of utilizing its extensive data and witness the next phase of growth. Popular use cases include the use of AI to enable trade promotion effectiveness. CPG companies use the Digilytics platform to collect data from past trade promotions, measure effectiveness based on return on investment (ROI), and make recommendations for future promotions based on calculated predictions. Product planning functions use AI-based systems to predict the quantity of product requirements and the delay in which SKUs need to be restocked. AI has also a major role to play in supply chain optimization. It can reduce manual efforts and increase efficiency in logistics. Digilytics' research has found that there are approximately 20 use cases which have been consistently taken up in the past decade by CI companies to enhance their business objectives. When these use cases are deployed at scale, these organizations have experienced a double-digit growth in business metrics.

## Selected Use Cases in Indian Market in Consumer Industries

Revenue growth challenges represent a large number of use cases for AI. These need to be addressed based on a deep understanding of customer behaviour through demand forecasting, optimizing promotion spends, customer segmentation, early customer attrition signals and supporting trade channels through secured lending. Given the very large number of SKUs and the wide geographic spread and channel stakeholders, a de-averaged view of revenue metrics is critical, but can be challenging to create. Additionally, there are other challenges such as product development, supply chain planning, store operations, campaign management and customer experience. Digilytics has gained experience in implementing some of these.

**Revenue Growth Enablers:** This use case provides insights about improved control over revenue metrics. Digilytics provides easy-to-use tools providing sales analyzer solutions for sales managers to navigate from diagnosis to actions. It provides an improved understanding of customer behaviour where it enables AI-based techniques to segment customers and develop unique growth strategies. It offers opportunities to upsell and cross-sell with early customer-level signals. This solution also has the ability to detect and address customer attrition and helps to deep dive into the comparative benchmark view across markets, customer segments and product categories of consumer companies in India. This sales analyzer tool also forecasts sales across all hierarchies (product, region, channel, etc.). Sales forecasting is a practical model combined with human intervention of the right set of behaviours impacting sales and accurately predicts future sales volumes. It supports improved decision making through structured scenario analysis.

**Secured Lending Automation**: This use case provides an opportunity to the finance department of any consumer company to play an active role in the financing of goods for their business stakeholders such as distributors and retailers. Companies provide trade finance/working capital loans to the retailers, and this process requires a lot of manual intervention in terms of verifying credibility of the debtor. Digilytics has developed AI tools to support loan origination by extracting data from documents and other unstructured sources and assisting rapid and low-cost disbursement of funds.

**Trade Promotion Optimisation**: A number of companies have developed systems, leveraging tools like the Digilytics platform, to identify the right price and discount point that maximises the sales lift and return on investment (RoI). These systems evaluate the success of promotions and the drivers behind it. As a result companies can easily gain insight into what they are executing according to the year's promotion plan and whether the trade promotion spend and discounts offered are in check with the planning and budget.

## Other Use Cases Gaining Popularity in Consumer Industries in India

1. **Product Assortment Intelligence**: This mechanism structures the product portfolio, taking into account several factors such as real-time pricing and competitors' product positioning. It helps to identify the right set of products, brands and categories where companies will have a unique advantage. They can quickly adjust their own product mix and pricing to make profitable pricing decisions and drive sales performance.

2. **Pricing Recommendation**: This use case helps companies understand the impact for a given change in pricing elasticity across products and similarly impact on contribution margin. It gives the organization a formidable position to take a lead in setting the right price points and gain a strong market share among its competitors.

3. **Market Mix Modelling**: This use case helps understand customer behaviour with regards to exposure to advertising. This model measures

the RoI of advertisements across various channels such as television, print and web. It results in a marketing RoI tracking system for an omnichannel partner, which builds a strong basis to target the most profitable customers.

## Improving Interaction with Retailers and End Consumers with the Help of AI

While a number of the use cases cited above involve the B2B part of CI businesses, the industry in India is also benefitting from the use of AI in interacting with the 10 million retailers and the billion consumers. This is more pronounced in newer brands selling to new-age consumers and new general trade and modern trade retailers. In June 2020, Reliance Jio, raised $7 billion of capital from technology majors like Facebook and Google, to digitally connect with the 10 million retailers and the 600 million mobile phone users in India. Their aspiration of creating digital interactions at scale is a great example of how the use of AI is rapidly increasing in the CI sector in India.

Additionally, brands are coming up with dynamic approaches to lure end consumers with redefined shopping experiences. Consumers have easy and quick accessibility to action-packed powered platforms such as smartphone assistants, chatbots and voice enabled devices. All these AI-based technologies have a pivotal role in influencing much of the customers' purchase decisions during their shopping journey. These platforms provide a personalized shopping experience to consumers with the right recommendations based on their past shopping behaviour. With busy schedules of the consumers, they do not have the requisite time to explore the products and are in a haste to make buying decisions. Here brands can play a significant role in engagement and cater to the consumers' intent for real, personalized and transparent communication in their buying experiences.

## Data-Led Strategy Adopted by Consumer Brands

Brands like Lenskart, Dabur, Titan and Jio have realized that data is the backbone for all informed decisions. They are in collaboration with most of the modern trade retailers for shopper data points to have a deeper understanding of omnichannel trends.

At the same time, given the fulfilment challenges in India, consumers still prefer in-store product purchase and collection, as it provides them with personalized in-store experiences and the chance to interact with store managers. This ensures that retailers largely control consumers' in-moment decisions. Because of this, most consumer companies do not get the opportunity to interact with consumers directly and to influence their purchasing patterns. Now there are emerging technologies where AI-enabled devices are being integrated with diagnostic capabilities to engage target customers in a truly immersive manner. Such new trends in technology is a win-win situation for both consumers and brands. Consumers experience enhanced shopping experience with more perceived value, personalization and convenience. On the other hand, brands are in a position to build a better emotional connection, by providing customization and real-time feedback to their consumers.

## Customer Success Stories in Indian Consumer Market

With the practices of AI implementation in the CI sector increasing, many companies have tasted success and refined their processes.

Titan is an Indian consumer goods company and is into the manufacturing of fashion accessories such as watches, jewellery and eyewear. Titan wanted to enhance their omnichannel presence in multiple cities of India. It has successfully taken its customer experience to the next level, such as buy online and pickup at store. From the application point of view, it has implemented machine learning (ML) across its 300+ stores pan-India in its sales forecasting system for jewellery business. The ML-based engine forecasts sales volume on the basis of structured data in the form of purchasing pattern and other retail statistics. The forecasting system has been built with customised modules for every individual business unit (watches, eyewear, jewellery, etc.) and store.

## Barriers to Implementing AI in Consumer Industries

While most senior executives are convinced of the benefits of the scaling up of AI and analytics in their organizations, they are also cautious about the fact that deploying the changes at a large scale brings change-management challenges, especially with large workforces in the sector. In general, the field force in this sector is less qualified and trained, compared to CI-sector workforce in developed markets like the United States and the UK. As a result, while technology adoption is quicker, given the younger demographic profile, training the workforce to effectively use the AI-enabled tools requires much higher levels of training, thereby slowing the change process. Digilytics' experience has proven that scaling up the use of AI applications is slow and time-consuming, and requires a significant amount of top-down sponsorship. To overcome this part, most companies adopt a pilot-based approach. Pilots are typically for a specific use case on a specific brand and in a specific region. Companies intending to adopt AI technology in India should take a five-step approach:

- Define a clear AI strategy: Set out clear objectives and targets of the business benefits to be delivered from the use of AI. Examine industry experience to define the strategy and prioritise use cases to be deployed.
- Ensure basic data quality: Understand the key internal and external data sources to be used for the use cases. Collate and structure the requisite data for AI-enabled applications. Define basic processes for data wrangling to ensure data quality, management and ownership.
- Build or buy the right talent: Understand that deploying AI technology requires niche skills (business analysts, data scientists, specialized engineers and data architects). Since this skillset is not core to CI companies, consider partnering with firms like Digilytics, who are able to supply this talent along with easy-to-use sector-specific AI tools.
- Create top-level sponsorship for adoption: Since the deployment and adoption is slow and effort-intensive, maintain continued top-management sponsorship. Celebrate early success of pilots to enable adoption.

## Digilytics as a Pioneer in Revenue Growth Management

Digilytics, is a pioneer in providing easy-to-use AI products for revenue growth management to the CI sector. Digilytics RevUp CI helps in:

1. improved understanding of customer behaviour:
   - AI-enabled techniques to segment customers and develop unique growth strategies
   - AI-enabled customer-level signals to detect opportunities to upsell and cross-sell
   - near-time signals to detect and address customer attrition
   - health of distribution networks: distributor reach, part reach, retailer reach and service reach
2. granular visibility of revenue underperformance
   - granular visibility and diagnostics of revenue performance
   - market share, product category, geography, channel partner, organisation
   - proactive intelligent assistance to highlight revenue underperformance
   - internal benchmarking across markets, customer segments and product categories

3. improved control over secondary sales
   - AI-enabled recommendations for market actions
   - easy-to-use assistive tools for sales managers to navigate from diagnosis to actions
   - share actionable insights and communicate with relevant individuals or groups
   - performance views to support near-time understanding of customer behaviour and market movements

Working with market leaders in consumer sector in India, Digilytics' experience reflects deep expertise in the broader CI sector in India.

## Selected Case Studies

1. One of the largest home-grown consumer company in India wanted to gain insight in trade promotion effectiveness through two key dimensions – promotional performance and promotional planning. Digilytics Revel CI was deployed to allow the company to evaluate trade promotion performance and the success of promotions and the drivers behind it. The tool also allowed the client to evaluate trade promotional planning. As a result they could easily gain insight into what they were executing according to the year's promotion plan and whether the trade promotion spends and discounts were in check with the planning and budget.
2. A renowned automobile manufacturer in India with its distribution across all states wanted to improve its market share in the aftermarket sales of automobile spare parts. Digilytics deployed its Revel CI tool to segment customers and develop unique growth strategies and attrition model to detect opportunities to upsell and cross-sell.

## AI in Other Sectors in India

The use of AI in India is not restricted to consumer industries. AI is rapidly gaining acceptance in financial services, healthcare and public services.

In financial services, AI is fuelling the growth of digital lending, which is expected to be a $1 trillion market by 2023. Typical use cases in digital lending include use of deep learning techniques to extract and validate information stored in documents for loan origination. Digilytics is one of the leaders in leveraging AI to super-charge the loan origination process. Improved risk management, pricing and the use of intelligent virtual assistants to enhance customer service are rapidly emerging as popular use cases of AI in financial services.

Similarly, in healthcare, AI is being used to improve public health and well-being. AI is being used by pharmaceutical companies and healthcare providers to understand disease trends and patterns and develop products and services to combat the most common diseases such as diabetes, hypertension and glaucoma. Digilytics is associated with a number of providers of AI-enabled products and services in this space.

Last, but not least, in public services, departments such as the police and national security rely heavily on AI to fight cybercrime, detect threat patterns and combat threats from terrorism.

## References

Aggarwal, Nikhar. (2020). The tech behind Titan's 99% accurate sales forecasting ET Cio. com. https://cio.economictimes.indiatimes.com/news/business-analytics/the-tech-behind-titans-99-accurate-sales-forecasting/73974462.

Brea, Cesar, Jeroen Hegge, Laurent Hermoye, Michael Jongeneel and Alejandro Navarro. (2019). From hype to hero: A look at artificial intelligence in the consumer packaged goods industry. https://www.bain.com/insights/from-hype-to-hero-a-look-at-artificial-intelligence-in-the-consumer-packaged-goods-industry/.

Charaborty, Dipita. (2020). The changed game for revenue growth management in CPG. https://fractal.ai/changed-game-for-revenue-growth-management-in-cpg/?utm_campaign=Article%20-%20The%20changed%20game%20for%20revenue%20growth%20management%20in%20CPG&utm_content=130706763&utm_medium=social&utm_source=linkedin&hss_channel=lcp-26945.

Charlin, Guillaume, Jeff Gell, Nicolas de Bellefonds, Taylor Smith, Vincent Lui, Julien Bellemare, Jimmy Royston, and Cindy Sehili. (2018). Unlocking growth in CPG with AI and advanced analytics. https://www.bcg.com/en-in/publications/2018/unlocking-growth-cpg-ai-advanced-analytics.

Nasscom. (2020). AI pervasiveness in retail. https://community.nasscom.in/wp-content/uploads/attachment/20195-ai-pervasiveness-in-retail-13-dec-2019.pdf.

PwC. (2016). PwC's analytics solutions for the FMCG sector. https://www.pwc.in/assets/pdfs/consulting/technology/data-and-analytics/pwcs-analytics-solutions-for-the-fmcg-sector.pdf.

Shah, Alpesh, Prateek Roongta, Shashank Avadhani and Dhruv Shah. (2018). Digital lending: A $1 trillion opportunity over the next 5 years, *Boston Consulting Group*. https://www.bcg.com/en-in/digital-lending-a-1-trillion-opportunity-over-the-next-5-years.

Srivastava, Priya. (2018). CPG industry gets a makeover for better consumer experience. https://www.indianretailer.com/article/technology/in-store/CPG-Industry-gets-a-makeover-for-better-consumer-experience.a5966/.

Udasi, Vijay, and Vikram Dhunta. (2016). Global MNCs and local giants: Winning in India. https://www.nielsen.com/wp-content/uploads/sites/3/2019/04/nielsen-report-global-mncs-and-local-giants-winning-in-india.pdf.

# Chapter 9

# "ALL-IN AI": WHAT IS COMPELLING COMPANIES IN CHINA TO BET THE HOUSE ON ARTIFICIAL INTELLIGENCE?

Dan Wong

## Introduction

It's very difficult to summarize a topic as deep as AI in a place a big as China. The objective of this chapter is to provide a snapshot of the current industry status as well as potential future developments, drawing heavily on the direct experience of the author. AI's 60-plus year history has been characterized by five to six waves of development and stagnation. Each wave has been driven by a new approach (such as expert systems or symbolic AI) which achieves breakthroughs in a specific area. This is followed by excitement, investment, and overexpectation followed almost inevitably by disappointment and abandonment. China has largely been absent from these waves of development, except the most recent cycle that started in the early 2010s. This wave has been driven by a new technology known as machine learning. It is unclear whether this new wave of development will meet the same fate as earlier cycles. Whatever the case, it's clear that China has already made big inroads in this area, both in terms of applications as well as research and development. China's entry into this phase of AI development has less to do with any particular expertise in machine learning and much more to do with the overall market and economic conditions of the country, which has enabled both private enterprises and government to invest significantly. No one could have anticipated that China would factor so heavily in the development of AI globally. Like many mega-trends, things began in a modest way.

## Humble Beginnings

Unlike the West, AI developments in China were initially driven by start-ups much more than the technology giants. This seems counterintuitive given the level of technological complexity and investment required. But China's tech landscape has historically been driven more by business models and operational innovation than investment in technology. In fact given the legal environment and often high degree of employee churn, it was often very difficult to protect any intellectual property or investments in research and development. Therefore, the first wave of Chinese technology companies were mainly consumer-focused internet companies such as Baidu, Alibaba, and Tencent (collectively known as "BAT") where sustained competitive advantage came through operations and implementation more than technology. The legal environment has improved significantly over the years, and there is no question that China's technology giants are investing heavily into research and development. However, the "DNA" of many established technology giants are not R&D-driven.

This is why in the summer of 2014, artificial intelligence (AI) was not on the agenda for most technology companies in China. Despite this situation, many entrepreneurs and scientists familiar with new developments in AI began to see the potential of applying this technology. It was during this general period of time (2012–14) that many of the "AI unicorns" in China started. It was also during this time that I had the fortune of becoming involved in this industry as the CEO of the start-up, Rokid. While the company never became a unicorn itself, Rokid's story is illustrative of how the AI industry evolved in China. Based out of Hangzhou, the company's dream was to apply AI to the smart home. At that time, Rokid was atypical in its employment of a large in-house team of PhDs for developing the voice recognition system that would form the basis of their product. At this stage in China's development, very few companies pursued such a path, and very few venture capital (VC) firms invested in purely technology-driven start-ups. However, this was already beginning to change. While AI was definitely not mainstream at the time, there were already Chinese VC firms and institutional investors actively searching for AI and robotics-based investments. As a result, Rokid and similar companies were able to obtain substantial funding fairly quickly. It was during this time that the "Four Dragons" of China's AI computer vision industry came into being: Sensetime, DeepGlint, Megvii, and Yitu. Voice recognition unicorns such as Mobvoi, Unisound, and AI-Speech were also founded around this same time. This "early mover" mentality of the investment and start-up community put China in an advantageous position for AI development.

My experience at Rokid provides some perspective on the market environ-ment during that time. After getting funding, I was in Silicon Valley in early 2015 to set up Rokid's US-based operations and research team. Since I spent the early part of my career in Silicon Valley, I used the opportunity to talk to VC and industry contacts on the ground. Without exception, each person discouraged me from pursuing AI, pointing out that the field has been in exist-ence for 60+ years without producing any unicorns or truly ground-breaking applications. While this is not strictly true, the example provides a snapshot into the prevailing attitude and conventional wisdom in Silicon Valley at the time. AI was not on the roadmap and not in the mainstream.

## Things Change Quickly

Things changed very quickly in late 2014 and early 2015, with several catalysts coming together at once. The big one was Amazon's announcement of Alexa and Echo on November 2014. Voice recognition powered by new machine learning algorithms appeared to take an important jump up in performance and accuracy. The team at Rokid were able to obtain a unit in early 2015 and were impressed with its performance, especially its far-field capabilities of accurately recognizing speech from several meters distance and under back-ground noise interference. Rokid was developing a similar technology, and Amazon's Echo helped to validate the approach. In the United States, many merely considered Echo to be an interesting product,. However in China, this invention ignited the imagination and excitement of consumers and industry in a way that may be hard to understand for those who haven't lived in China. Products immediately started flooding the market, and new AI start-ups appeared to be getting funded daily. This was a new breed of company, willing to invest in technology as a competitive advantage. Given the flush funding environment at the time, many AI technology companies were seeded and started.

Even the China technology incumbents started to wake up to the fact that they needed to invest more in technology. Baidu was one of the earliest to make serious investments into AI. It set up its first AI and Machine Learning Research Center in 2013. In 2016, Baidu recruited AI pioneer Andrew Ng as its chief scientist to bring its capabilities to the next level. As cofounder of Google Brain, and professor and director of Stanford's AI Lab, Andrew was a recognized global heavyweight. News of his hire energized the China tech scene. At the subsequent 2016 Baidu World Event, founder and CEO Robin Li announced that AI was the "Core of the Core." The following year in 2017, Baidu officially announced their "All-In AI" strategy.

Actually, there is an important underlying reason for this trend toward deeper technology investments: the shift in market dynamics from business-to-consumer (B2C) to business-to-business (B2B) products and services. The common wisdom, especially for the technology giants, was that B2C had run its course in China and had reached a bottleneck. Customer acquisition costs through online channels had reached a level approaching offline acquisition costs. The next engine for growth needed to be B2B. And in the case of B2B business, technology is a critical competitive advantage.

Tencent, the inventor of China's ubiquitous super app WeChat, was one of the first to make that shift by announcing a major organization restructuring in 2018. This was their first reorganization in six years and was designed to transition the company from B2C to B2B, positioning them for the next twenty years where "ABC" (AI, big data, and cloud) would be decisive competitive advantages.

With typical China speed, all the incumbents started to create service offerings tailored to a broad range of industry verticals. One of the common ingredients in this technology arsenal was AI.

## China Speed, Scale, and Access to Data

When I first moved to China in 2003, the country was still an "emerging" market. What this meant was that China drove a very small portion of actual business for most multinationals, and most local companies were dwarfed by their international counterparts in scale. In reality, many companies were taking a "wait-and-see" attitude toward investments in China.

At the time, there was much debate about whether China had potential as a consumer market. Certainly it had a very large population, but the spending power was so low that there was no market. At that time, China's economy was principally export-driven. No one would have imagined the day that China would become one of the world's largest consumer markets, with Chinese consumers buying up to a third of the world's luxury goods. My experience at Nokia mirrored this rapid development. From 2003 through 2008, I managed Nokia's high-end N-Series product line for Greater China. At the time, Nokia's N-Series sales were split into five sales areas globally. In 2003, China was second to last in terms of revenue and profit contribution, which was understandable given that N-Series devices could cost up to US$800 to – US$1000 per unit. When the company reorganized in 2008, China was the largest sales area, with an annual run-rate of US$1.9B.

This explosion of China's consumer market was mirrored in all sectors, and it is this consumer scale that has become one of the first critical foundations for the development of AI in China. To the extent that AI needs data to enhance its performance, China's massive consumer market has provided the raw fuel to power the machine learning models behind AI. There are few countries in the world with similar size of market and amount of data generated. This has allowed AI applications to improve at an incredible rate. With the government as the biggest customer for applications such as security, the industry started to witness Chinese companies like SenseTime and Yitu beating international technology giants in premier global competitions like CVPR and ImageNet. The availability of data allowed China to leap from "backwater" to "center stage" in an amazingly short period of time.

## China-Style Innovation and the Development of AI: "Crossing the River while Feeling for Stones"

To the extent that AI and machine learning are about experimentation and heuristics, there is another aspect of China's market environment that has benefited AI. There is a saying in Chinese, "crossing the river while feeling for stones." For a very long time in China's history, there was a severe lack of expertise across multiple industry domains and fields of study. Very often, the only option to get something done was by trial-and-error. In other words, crossing the river first and then feeling your way along. While it is not stated explicitly in Chinese technology circles, this ethos has been central to the way companies innovate in this market. In fact, this mentality has freed many entrepreneurs from being tied down by preconceived notions, theories, and approaches. They are willing to try sometimes crazy ideas that may not see the light of day in other markets. Because of China's development history, this habit of "feeling for stones" is deeply embedded in the psyche. Whether it is the entrepreneurs themselves or their employees, customers, and investors, there is a willingness to try new things. In most other countries around the world, investors would likely not allow their portfolio companies to start doing things completely unrelated or beyond their focus areas. This feeling for stones approach has led to many failures, but it has also led to new types of innovation not seen elsewhere and which is starting to expand from China to other regions.

One example is the emergence of the Super App, an app that is all things to all people. In places like Silicon Valley, the conventional wisdom has been that pursuing this is a dead-end path. No company is able to master multiple fields. In fact, Silicon Valley's basic 0-to-1 innovation playbook is to focus deeply in one area only, an approach known as MVP (minimum viable product). While many Chinese technology companies say they are doing MVP, my observation is that they are in fact doing something very different. These companies are actually pursuing "boundary-less" innovation, where they jump across seemingly unrelated fields. Meituan Dianping's CEO Wang Xing is one of the first to verbalize this approach, and his company is one of the most successful technology companies in China.

This type of boundary-less experimentation is very much in line with the nature of AI. AI is driven by machine learning, where there is a continuous iteration of data input compared to outputs. Very often the results are not what is expected and hard to explain by any specific theory or model. Therefore the speed of learning, iteration, and experimentation are critical factors in the successful application of AI in practice. In other words, there is an advantage to not being tied down by a specific mindset and approach. Being able to move rapidly and flexibly across different paths is a critical success factor as it relates to AI. This is one of the reasons why some experts say that China may take the lead in applying AI to real-life applications, even though it may still lag other countries in terms of fundamental and basic research.

## The Rallying Effect of Government for AI Development

I remember my first meetings with government officials and state-owned enterprises (SOE's) in China. It was 2001 and my Silicon Valley based company, Openwave Corporation, was one of the premier solution providers for a technology known as WAP (Wireless Access Protocol), which enabled mobile devices to access the internet. The company's biggest customers were the global telecommunications services providers. As the product manager, I made a trip to Beijing in early 2001 to meet with operator customers. I was immediately struck by the tone and approach of the entire meeting. Openwave had prepared a comprehensive proposal, with business case, financials, and implementation considerations. The senior executives at the meeting appeared not to care about this and instead asked predominately noneconomic and policy-level questions. At the end of the meeting, they instructed the team to communicate several key messages to the US government. Frankly, I didn't really know what to do with these "non-business" issues and not even sure who in the US government to contact. In my many years working in Silicon Valley, I seldom gave any serious thought about how to coordinate or get feedback from the government. Rules were generally quite clear and actions were driven by commercial considerations, as they should be. This was not and is not the case in China. Government policy and attitude are often the first items that companies consider before starting new projects or investing and deploying new services, products, and technologies.

At those Beijing meetings, the people were all senior executives at China's three major telecommunications providers (China Mobile, China Telecom, China Unicom), all publicly listed entities. While this was the case, personnel appointments at the VP level and above were in fact made by the Organization Department of the Central Committee of the Communist Party of China (CCCPC). Therefore, senior executives had a dual role to safeguard the business viability of their enterprises and also to implement government policy, often with government policy having a more significant impact on promotions and job security than commercial success. Nowhere was this clearer than when in 2006, the government announced that the CEOs of all three telecommunications providers would switch places. In this management musical chairs, the CEO of China Unicom became the CEO of China Mobile, the CEO of China Mobile become the CEO of China Telecom, and the CEO of China Telecom became the CEO of China Unicom. This was quite an amazing situation, because each of these companies were fierce competitors to one another in the marketplace. Clearly, factors other than financial performance drove that decision. The same thing happened again in 2015 when the CEOs of China Unicom and China Telecom switched places, and the CEO of China Mobile was replaced by an ex-vice minister of the Ministry of Industry and Information Technology (MIIT).

The hand of government is visible across all businesses in China, in a way that is not necessarily the case in other markets. There are certainly issues and shortcomings to this approach. However, in the case of driving development in new technologies such as AI, the direction set by the government has a very powerful impact in terms of focusing resources, funding, and activities because all players are very attuned to the policy and direction set by the government.

Much has been made about the rallying impact of the Chinese government for AI. Many tend to focus on the funding made available. Actually in many cases, the announced funding comes in the form of tax breaks, subsidies, matching funds, and other forms, and is often not as large as it may appear in the media. Oftentimes, it is private enterprises such as VC and private equity (PE) firms that step in. They are willing to do this, because government policy de-risks these new initiatives for VC and PE investors, who then come into the market based on a pure-profit motive. In this way, the interaction between government and private enterprise becomes a mutually reinforcing cycle. In many ways, the behaviour of the Chinese government itself is almost like a VC firm. They are willing to make bets and "feel for stones" on new technology development, because the overall trend has been benefit over downside. The Chinese government often takes a permissive attitude in the beginning and only regulates after things get to scale. This very unique blend of capitalism and planned economy is seldom seen elsewhere.

The Chinese government has made no secret about the importance of AI to national policy and strategy. In 2017, the government announced an ambitious plan to take leadership in this critical technology domain, with three targets: By 2020, China will reach global parity in terms of overall technology and applications in AI. By 2025, the country will realize major breakthroughs in fundamental science as well as world leadership in some application areas. The year 2030 targets global leadership in AI theory, technology, and applications. China will become a leading global innovation center for AI.

## AI Is a "Must-Have"

In the past three decades, an entire population has been lifted out of poverty: a total of 850 million as estimated by the World Bank. With the burden of 1.4 billion people, multitudes of pressing issues require solutions. Cities suffer from extreme congestion. There are long lines at banks, border crossings, and government offices. The healthcare system is overwhelmed in big cities while basic services are lacking in second tier and smaller cities. Education faces similar challenges from K to 12 and beyond. The past 30 years of China's economic transformation has directly benefited from technology advancement and adoption, leading to a belief that technology will continue to be a linchpin of the country's growth and success.

For the United States and many countries, AI is a "nice-to-have." For China, AI is a "must have." The country needs a technology like AI to solve the serious issues it faces. The speed and scope at which China has changed requires a technology that can address issues quickly and broadly. AI fits the bill, because it can deal with massive amounts of data and be applied across a broad range of industries and settings. This is the reason that China must go "All-In" on AI.

There is probably no industry as far removed from AI technology as construction cranes, machinery, and equipment. In June 2019, I had the chance to visit Zoomlion in Changsha, China, on behalf of an AI company I was advising. Zoomlion was founded in 1992 and ranks as China's second (and the world's sixth) largest construction machinery enterprise. Before the visit, I was skeptical of Zoomlion's reasons and commitments for investing in AI technology. Over Long-Jing tea and Cuban cigars with their chairman and senior management team on the roof of their headquarters, they explained why Zoomlion needed to go 'all-in' on AI. The competitive pressure and speed of the market meant they could not rest on their laurels. Even though they had been market leaders for a long period of time, they felt a true sense of urgency. In fact, Zoomlion was in the process of making a "bet the company" move. Over the next five years, they planned to invest roughly $100B RMB (US$14B) to build a fully automated, AI-driven "Intelligence Factory City." They would not give themselves a backup plan by retaining their existing production facilities, which would be phased out completely. All production would move to this new 900,000 square meter facility. In addition, they had already set up their own AI Research Lab in collaboration with Andrew Ng's Landing.ai to ensure that they build their own internal capabilities at a global level of excellence. The story of Zoomlion is a window into the way AI is quickly being adopted across all sectors in China, with a speed that is often breathtaking.

## The AI "Splinterverse"?

At the time of this writing, it is not clear what will happen to the underlying technology foundations of AI. As described in this book, AI innovation and research is happening across all countries globally. When AI was first applied in China, no one would have guessed that China could rival the United States and other countries in terms of AI development. In the years afterwards, things have changed rapidly. Many say that China has taken the lead in the application of AI technology, especially in terms of consumer-facing applications, even though it still lags in terms of fundamental research.

Given that much of the newest AI research is being conducted in the United States, there used to be a saying that the distance between China and Silicon Valley in terms of AI technological development is 15 hours. This is the time difference between California and China. The AI industry has a very deep academic tradition, where new research and findings are published and publicly shared on sites such as arXiv.org. Fifteen hours is the time it would take for a paper to be published and when someone in China could read and study the same paper. Of course, not all information is shared, and technology giants keep many of their core findings confidential. But compared to other industries, AI is a field that relies much more on collaboration and shared research.

At the time of this writing, the US and China relationship is at a low point. Many Chinese AI companies are on the US Entity List, which means that companies are prohibited from providing "US-originated" core technologies to them. There has always been a "parallel universe" in terms of the software technology stack in China, with a Great Firewall around China's internet that prevents users from accessing sites and services outside. However, the underlying "plumbing" and building blocks for these Chinese internet services have been largely the same as those outside: using the same IC chips, programming language, tools, and frameworks as their international counterparts. As an example, the most commonly used AI framework in China is Google's Tensorflow, even though Google's consumer-facing services such as Google Search and Maps are not available in China. Some say that this situation is

China's "house of cards," with the foundation highly reliant on external technology and therefore susceptible to disruptions or embargos.

There is a fork in the road ahead. It's not clear whether future development of AI will diverge or come back together at some point in the future. Certainly, the Chinese government, investors, and industry participants are making significant investments in indigenous technologies to reduce external dependency. This means the parallel universe will split even more deeply. For users and businesses, it would seem that an "AI Splinterverse" would be an unfortunate development. As we look forward, it appears that the key determining factors are geopolitical, rather than technological or economic, in nature. If AI services can fulfil their promise of looking into the future, perhaps it will be they that produce the wisdom to tell us humans what to do next.

# Chapter 10

# ARTIFICIAL INTELLIGENCE RESEARCH IN RUSSIA: RECOVERING FROM THE POLAR WINTER

Oleg P. Kuznetsov and Sergei O. Kuznetsov

## First Decades: The Soviet Era

As of now, Russian researchers do not typically make the lists of major newsmakers when it comes to Artificial Intelligence (AI). However, this trend is being rapidly reversed, and the home country of the first world champion in computer chess games and inventors of the mathematical learning theory will soon very likely catch up with the very best in both the academia and the industry.

The first attempts at what can be called "AI before AI" can be traced back to the 1820s to 1830s Russia, when, concurrently with Ada Lovelace, Semyon N. Korsakov proposed a series of mechanical machines for "enhancing natural intelligence" through "comparison of ideas" (Karsakoff 1832) to the Imperial Academy of Science in St. Petersburg. In modern terms, Korsakov's ideoscope could compute set-theoretic intersection and complement (which gives a complete set of Boolean functions) over data given by object-attribute tables implemented by punched cards. Unlike Jaccard machines driven by programs on punched cards—the precursors of machines with numerical control—Korsakov's ideoscope was intended for information processing with symbolic computation, such as checking the similarity, difference, search, and classification. Like toy steam engines designed in ancient Greece, these inventions were hardly technologically scalable and did not meet societal needs of the day, so they sank into oblivion till the rise of the computer era in the 1950s.

It is worth mentioning that Soviet and Russian researchers of the twentieth century would often not claim that they "were doing AI," so our classification follows the modern view of what is AI. AI, as a striking term motivating better fund raising in Western countries, was under suspicion (not always ideological) in Soviet science, which tried to keep to deeper-grounded nomenclature of science branches, with a sort of Arbor Porphyriana as the archetype of classification of things. In 1954, two years before the now-famous Dortmund seminar, where the name Artificial Intelligence was coined, A. A. Lyapunov started his seminar "Automata and Thinking" at Moscow State University. The event featured physiologists, linguists, psychologists, and mathematicians, and arguably marked the start of AI research in Soviet Russia. Back in the day, AI was considered as a branch of cybernetics. In 1954, A. A. Lyapunov launched a machine translation project at the Mathematical Institute of Soviet Academy of Science. One of the participants of this project was I. A. Mel'čuk, who, together with Yu. D. Apresyan, later developed the famous Meaning-Text Theory (Mel'čuk 1981). Another machine translation project was launched in the mid-1950s at the Lebedev Institute for Precision Mechanics and Computer Engineering.

In the 1950s and 1960s, at the Leningrad (now St. Petersburg) Department of Mathematical Institute of the Academy of Sciences, research on automated theorem proving was conducted. Specifically, researchers developed strategies of "inverse method" by Yu. S. Maslov, which is similar to logical resolution by J. Robinson. Some important steps in designing methods of pattern recognition were made during the 1950s and 1960s by M. N. Vaintsvaig and M. M. Bongard (CORA algorithm, Institute of Information Transmission Problems) in Moscow and by N. G. Zagoruiko at Novosibirsk University (in his school on "Automatic recognition of audio images").

In 1960–61, E. M. Braverman put forward the famous "compactness hypothesis" for pattern recognition. In 1965–71, E. M. Braverman, together with V. A. Aizerman and L. I. Rozonoer (Institute for Control Sciences, ICS), developed the method of potential functions, which under the name of "kernel functions" became machine learning classics. The Yu. I. Zhuravlev school of pattern recognition based on logical testers and algorithms computing estimates started in the mid-1960s. In the 1960s, V. N. Vapnik and A. Ya. Chervonenkis from ICS proved their prominent condition of uniform convergence of frequency to probability, which underlies the Theory of Learnable rediscovered by L. G. Valiant in the 1980s. Their results led to the development of the concept of Vapnik-Chervonenkis (VC) dimension and Support Vector Machine (SVM) method.

At the same time, M. L. Tsetlin at the Keldysh Institute for Applied Mathematics studied biologically inspired goal-oriented behavior of automata in random media, laying the groundwork for automata learning and reinforcement learning (Tsetlin 1973). Meanwhile, at the Kiev Institute for Cybernetics, V. M. Glushkov developed machine learning approaches to the analysis of meaningfulness of sentences and texts. He also introduced the notion of semantic networks. In the mid-1960s, D. A. Pospelov started his research on situational control and applied semiotics. In 1974, the scientific panel on AI was founded at the Soviet Academy of Sciences, with G. S. Pospelov as president and D. A. Pospelov as co-president.

As for the development of robotics, it started within the Soviet space industry. The first achievements came to light in the early 1960s, when a group from Bauman Technical University equipped the Vostok spacecraft with the first outer manipulator. Fifteen intelligent robots saved thousands of lives when fixing the damage caused by the Chernobyl disaster in 1986 (this fact was overlooked in the 2019 hit TV series on Chernobyl).

By 1975, when V. L. Stefanuk organized the International Joint Conference on Artificial Intelligence (IJCAI) for the first (and only) time in the Soviet Union (Tbilisi, now Georgian Republic), Soviet research in AI had shown some remarkable results, including the chess-playing program KAISSA (by a team of M. G. Adelson-Velsky and V. L. Arlazarov, ICS), which became the first world champion among chess-playing systems in 1974. About 20 percent of papers accepted for IJCAI-1975 came from Soviet researchers, mostly from Moscow, Leningrad (St. Petersburg), Kiev, and Novosibirsk.

Several series of conferences were organized, like Semiotic Aspects of Formalizing Intelligent Activity (since 1983), Mathematical Methods of Pattern Recognition (since 1983), Machine Discovery of Regularities (since 1976), and so on.

The research of D. A. Pospelov in adaptive collective behavior, situational control, applied semiotics, and cognitive semantics made AI popular among Soviet researchers and laypeople, linking AI models and different phenomena in science, technology, the humanities, and culture (see, e.g., Pospelov 1981, 1987).

Since 1981, the team of V. K. Finn at VINITI Institute of the Academy of Sciences (Moscow) began developing the JSM-method of hypothesis generation inspired by F. Bacon's and J. S. Mill's schemes of inductive reasoning.

During 1980–90, Alexander N. Gorban's (Gorban and Rossiev 1990) team researched into neural networks at the Computer Center of the Siberian Branch of the Academy of Sciences (Krasnoyarsk). In Novosibirsk, Yu.L. Ershov and S. S. Goncharov (later D. E. Palchunov) started the study of logico-semantic foundations of AI.

In 1988, the first Soviet Conference on AI was held in Pereslavl-Zalessky, drawing over two hundred participants.

Starting in the mid-1980s, the technological gap between USSR and Western countries became obvious. One of the reasons was that in the late 1960s, instead of supporting outstanding original computer development, Soviet authorities opted to have computer production unified based on borrowings from IBM architecture. Early research conducted by the enthusiasts of the 1950s and 1960s was not seeing enough support from the industry and society. Lacking computer resources, many research projects reached a standstill.

In the 1990s, research activity in Russian AI hit the skids due to the dramatic economic downturn caused by the collapse of the Soviet Union. Many talented researchers left the country—the "AI winter" in post-Soviet Russia was quite palpable. Still, some new research groups teamed up and research conferences appeared in the academy, for example, the series of conferences on neurocomputers and their applications started in 1995 (with precursor conferences since 1988), initiated by A. I. Galushkin.

At this dramatic juncture, in a time of heavily underpaid jobs, scarce resources, and an absence of new international journals and books in libraries (a particularly painful experience in the pre-internet era), the Russian Association (Soviet Association in 1989–91) for AI fostered scientific interactions, intercollegiate research-related communication, and the exchange of ideas by organizing conferences (e.g., Russian Conference for AI; Pospelov Readings) and workshops and publishing new journals (*AI News, AI and Decision Making*), which helped many young people progress with their academic careers at least up until they could obtain their PhDs. Research during this period was socially motivated by an informal approval of the community and cannot be judged by modern bibliometric criteria. Prominent figures of the time (besides those mentioned above) include A. N. Averkin, I. Z. Batyrshin, S. M. Kovalev, V. B. Tarasov, N. G. Yarushkina (soft computing), A. P. Eremeev, V. K. Finn, V. N. Vagin (plausible reasoning), T. A. Gavrilova (knowledge bases and knowledge engineering), V. I. Gorodetsky (multiagent systems), V. F. Khoroshevsky (semantic technologies and analysis of research trends), A. S. Kleshchev (knowledge bases, ontologies), B. A. Kobrinsky (AI in medicine), L. T. Kuzin (knowledge bases), O. P. Kuznetsov (holographic memory and resource networks), G. S. Osipov (knowledge bases and applied semiotics), V. E. Pavlovsky (robotics), K. V. Rudakov, and K. V. Vorontsov (machine learning and pattern recognition), E. V. Popov, and G. V. Rybina (industrial intelligent systems).

## New Wave of AI Research in Russia

Things began to change in the mid-2000s, when, besides well-known research centers that had existed previously, such as the Russian Academy of Sciences, Moscow State University, and Novosibirsk University, new centers started shaping up. Several new Russian software companies, such as Yandex and ABBYY, boosted the new wave of AI research, now strongly oriented at practical results and production. In the 2010s, the main research focus on AI shifted to artificial neural networks, machine learning, computer vision, natural language processing (NLP), and their industrial applications. Quite recently, the demand for explainable AI has become more obvious, empowering the revival of research in logic-based AI.

## Academia

The (far from complete) list of Russian universities leading in the field of AI includes Moscow State University (MSU), Skoltech (Moscow), Moscow Institute of Physics and Technology (MIPT), National Research University Higher School of Economics (HSE, Moscow, St. Petersburg, Nizhny Novgorod), ITMO University (St. Petersburg), Tomsk State University, St. Petersburg State University, Novosibirsk State University, and Innopolis (Kazan). All these schools have close ties to the industry, with AI-intensive IT companies running industrial departments, which help them both teach advanced science and technology courses and attract talented young employees. In 2007, Yandex started its School for Data Analysis, a two-year master's level curriculum.

The list of oft-cited AI researchers (with over three thousand citations on Google Scholar, we refer only to researchers with main affiliations in Russia) looks as follows: A. Cichocki (Skoltech, image and signal processing), V. S. Lempitsky (Skoltech, computer vision), B. G. Mirkin (Higher School of Economics (HSE), clustering, classification), S. I. Nikolenko (St. Petersburg PDMI RAS, machine learning), I. V. Oseledets (Skoltech, tensor train for machine learning), T. A. Gavrilova (St. Petersburg State University, knowledge engineering), S. O. Kuznetsov (HSE, knowledge discovery, formal concept analysis), V. F. Khoroshevsky (knowledge engineering) D. P. Vetrov (HSE, deep learning, Bayesian inference), N.V. Loukachevitch (Moscow State University [MSU], NLP, linguistic ontologies), and A. A. Karpov (St. Petersburg Institute for Informatics and Automation of RAS (SPII RAS), speech recognition). AI- and ML-based approaches became efficient tools in natural science, like physics and biology. Here is a (not complete) list of highly cited Russian researchers applying ML approaches in these areas: A. E. Ustyuzhanin (HSE, high energy physics), A. R. Oganov (Skoltech, crystallography), A. E. Hramov (Innopolis, nonlinear dynamics), and M. V. Fedorov (Skoltech, chemical physics, molecular biophysics).

## Russian Conferences on AI

Russian Conference on AI (Springer proceedings); Dialog; Mathematical Methods of Pattern Recognition; Intelligent Data Processing: Theory and

Applications; Knowledge, Ontologies, Theories (KONT); Analysis of Images, Social Networks and Texts (AIST) (Springer proceedings), Fuzzy Systems and Soft Computing, Mathematical Methods of Pattern Recognition, Intelligent Data Processing, AI Journey; AVRA days; OpenTalks.AI; Machines Can See; Vision Technology Russia, Practical Aspects of AI technologies. Special mentions deserve the RCAI being the oldest conference, and OpenTalk.AI (organized annually by I. O. Pivovarov), the youngest one, which became a very popular forum (more than a thousand participants in 2020) bringing together academia and industry.

*Russian Journals with AI as core topic*

*AI and Decision Making, AI News, Fuzzy Systems and Soft Computing,* and *Pattern Recognition and Image Analysis.*

*Russian Associations in AI*

Russian Association for Artificial Intelligence, Russian Association for Neuroinformatics, Russian Association for Fuzzy Systems and Soft Computing, Russian Neuronet, Open Data Science, AI community, and Science Guide.

## Industry

The main industrial drivers of modern AI research in Russia are Yandex and Sberbank. Yandex originally started as an AI-intensive company, while Sberbank has been building its expertise in AI since about 2016. The Mail.ru Group Holding started AI research later, but reached third place in the unofficial rankings.

Among companies with focused research directions, the most noteworthy are Cognitive Technologies in pattern recognition and software for driver-free cars, Kaspersky for research in cybersecurity, ABBYY in OCR and NLP, IQ'men (Rostelecom) in trend prediction, and Speech Technology Center (STC) in developing software for voice and face recognition.

According to a recent SAP research (SAP 2019), some 1,400 AI scientific projects were carried out in Russia between 2007 and 2017. Most of them (1,200) were non-profit. In the past five years, however, the private sector has showed much more interest in the development and use of AI. Now AI applications in Russia are found in different areas: services personalization (e.g., telecom), efficiency increase by data analysis in retail and industry (e.g., telecom, home appliances, oil well drilling, banking), automation and optimization of technical support and communication by bots (e.g., food retail, telecom), assistance with and advice on companies' products (e.g., air tickets retail), HR and personnel recruitment, computer vision, augmented reality (AR), robotics, image recognition (text and documentation procession and analysis), video recognition (advertisement targeting), quality assurance in manufacturing processes (e.g., in the pharmaceutical industry) and so on.

## Natural Language Processing

Here, the leaders among IT companies are as follows (Almanac, no.2, 2019): Yandex: machine translation, speech recognition and synthesis, virtual assistants (e.g., "Alisa" with a user count of about 50 million monthly), information retrieval, and crowdsourced NLP projects for text mining.

Center of Speech Technologies (CST): voice and face biometry, speech recognition, speech synthesis, voice navigator, phone call analysis, and voice assistants.

ABBYY: Optical character recognition (OCR), intelligent retrieval, text mining and classification, intelligent platforms for business process analysis.

Mail.ru: intelligent retrieval, voice and image recognition, voice assistants, recommendation systems, and text mining.

Sberbank: decision support, speech services, chatbots, automated speech menu, preparation of legal documents, processing claims and complaints.

Some other leading companies include Just AI (speech processing), PROMT (machine translation, text mining), Tinkoff (speech processing), Nanosemantics (speech recognition and synthesis), Brand Analytics (text mining, trend detection), RCO (text mining), ACM Solutions (speech processing), Medialogy (semantic analysis, monitoring conventional and social media), Kribrum (SNA), MTS (speech processing), Naumen (knowledge management, chatbots).

## Computer Vision (CV, Almanac, no.3, 2020)

Yandex: Yandex Vision is a service for CV including OCR technology, moderation of content, and human recognition. Image retrieval performs better than similar functions in Google, Bing, and Baidu.

VisionLabs: image and object recognition based on neural networks.

NTech Labs: image, silhouette and action recognition in videos, mostly for security purposes.

Vocord: intelligent transport systems, video surveillance and video analytics, which involve recognition of license plates, moving objects, and various types of activities.

Mail.ru: CV for retail: access control based on recognition of customers' faces, CV for document processing and technological processes.

ABBYY: a world-leading company in OCR, recognition of hand-written text (ICR), optical mark recognition (OMR), and optical bar (code) recognition (OBR). Famous products include ABBYY FineReader Engine (OCR and ICR in applications), Mobile Capture, and Flexicapture, a universal platform for intelligent information processing.

Other leading companies in CV are Tevian (video surveillance and access control, document recognition), 3DiVi (augmented reality (AR), the IoT, robotics, biometrics), GosNIIAS (CV in aviation systems, biometrics), Cognitive Technologies (CV for driverless vehicles and drones in agriculture and railways) and so forth.

### National Russian Strategy in AI and Ethics of AI

Following general concerns about the social implications of AI technologies, in 2018, UNESCO started a discussion of recommendations on the ethics of AI. A committee of Russian AI experts and members of governmental bodies took part in designing the recommendations. Specific features of the position of the Russian Federation consist in stressing sovereignty of AI research policy of individual UNESCO member states and rejecting subjectivity (legal personality) of intelligent systems, which would have resulted in passing on to society the risks caused by manufacturers of autonomous intelligent systems.

In October 2019, the Office of the Russian President released a national AI strategy until 2030. AI technologies will have to contribute to the efficiency of planning, forecasting, and decision-making by management structures and individuals, automation of a significant part of routine production operations, improve safety and reduce risks of business processes, meet consumer demands, improve quality of public services, including medical services, education, and governmental and municipal services. Fundamental scientific research should be targeted at creating general (strong) AI, with a focus on biologically inspired approaches, machine learning, adaptive solutions, autonomous decomposition of problems, search and synthesis of decisions.

In 2020 the Russian government launched a program on designing state standards that would specify safety of AI applications for humans and the environment in various domains, including transport, medicine, education, construction, and so on.

To sum up, we would say that Soviet and Russian researchers made a substantial contribution to the foundation of modern AI technologies, but Russian AI industry has still to find its place on the local and international markets. We expect a new wave of fundamental results in AI that would bring new types of technologies based on a deeper understanding of the human brain and the biological mechanisms, with Russian researchers taking active part in international collaborations.

## Acknowledgments

The research of Sergei O. Kuznetsov leading to this publication has received funding from the Basic Research Program at the National Research University Higher School of Economics.

## References

Almanac AI, nos. 1–4. (2018–20). Center for Competence Research at Moscow Institute for Physics and Technology (MIPT), Moscow.

Bongard, M. M. (1970). Pattern recognition. Rochelle Park: Hayden Book.

Finn, V. K. (1983). On machine-oriented formalization of plausible reasoning in style of F. Bacon-J. S. Mill, *Semiotika I Informatika*, no. 20: 35–104 [in Russian].

Gaaze-Rappoport, M. G., and Pospelov, D. A. (1987). *From Amoeba to Robot: Models of Behavior*. Moscow: Nauka [in Russian].

Gavrilova, T. A., and Khoroshevsky, V. F. (2000). *Knowledge Bases of Intelligent Systems*. St. Petersburg: Piter.

Gorban, A. N., and Rossiev, D. A. (1990). *Neural networks on personal computer*. Novosibirsk: Nauka, p. 276.

Karsakof, S. (1832). *Apercu d'un procede nouveau d'investigation au moyen de machines a comparer les idees*. St. Petersburg: Imperial Academy of Science.

Kuznetsov, S. O. (2005). Galois Connections in Data Analysis: Contributions from the Soviet Era and Modern Russian Research. Formal Concept Analysis 2005, Berlin: Springer: pp. 196–225.

Mel'čuk, I. A. (1981). Meaning-text models: A recent trend in Soviet linguistics. *Annual Review of Anthropology*, vol. 10: 27–62.

Oseledets, I. V. (2011). Tensor-train decomposition. *SIAM J.Sci.Comp*, 33: 2295–317.

Osipov, G. S. (2011). *Methods of AI*. Moscow: Fizmatlit [in Russian].

Pospelov, D. A. (1981). *Logico-Linguistc Models in Control Systems*. Moscow: Energoatomizdat [in Russian].

Proc. 8th International Conference on Analysis of Images, Social Networks and Texts (AIST-2019), van der Aalst et al. (eds.), Springer LNCS 11832.

Proc. 18th Russian Conference on Artificial Intelligence (RCAI). (2020). S. O. Kuznetsov, A. I. Panov and K. S. Yakovlev (eds), Berlin: Springer.

SAP. (2019). Review. https://www.rvo.nl/sites/default/files/2019/07/Artificial-intelligence-in-Russia.pdf.

Shumsky, S. A. (2020). *Machine Intelligence*. Moscow: RIOR [in Russian].

Tsetlin, M. L. (1973). *Automation Theory and Modeling of Biological Systems*. Cambridge, MA: Academic Press.

Vapnik, V. N., and Chervonenkis, A. Ya. (1974). *Theory of Pattern Recognition (Statistical Problems of Learning)*. Moscow: Nauka [in Russian].

# Chapter 11

# THE FOURTH INDUSTRIAL REVOLUTION IN AFRICA

Wesley Doorsamy, Babu Sena Paul and Tshilidzi Marwala

## Introduction

We are now entering a new era of socio-economic disruption arising from the fourth industrial revolution (4IR) – which is characterized by the amalgamation of the digital, biological and physical realms (Ndung'u and Signé 2020). A key question on the African agenda is how Africa can leverage 4IR for its benefit and not miss out this time around. This chapter deals with this question and explores some of the crucial cross-cutting issues surrounding the topic of 4IR in the African context. This work is intended to serve as a high-level African perspective of the fourth industrial revolution that will assist scholars, policy-makers, researchers, governments, business and other stakeholders in their respective roles in taking Africa forward.

Technologies of the 4IR are perhaps not a far-off vision for Africa (AfDB 2019), and are already playing a pivotal role as Africa transitions into the mainstream global economy. There are ongoing developments across the continent with recent expansions by tech giants such as Netflix, Facebook, Google and so on into Africa, and the rapid growth of tech start-ups and other such exciting developments in Africa's emerging technology landscape (Bright 2016). It has become clear that industries and governments must invest in and leverage 4IR technologies to make gains in the modern-day global economy (Marwala 2019). Although there has been some positive movement on the continent, with improved human development indices, and better regional interactions and economic progress, there are very deep concerns about the continent potentially missing out on reaping the growth benefits of 4IR due to the lack of human capacity development, adequate infrastructure and coherent leadership (Mead 2017; Radu 2020). These major thematic areas, that is, infrastructure, human capacity development and policy are explored in this chapter in the context of Africa's preparedness for 4IR. Taking into account that Africa is a vast and diverse continent, a high-level analysis of these issues is carried out with emphasis placed on the critical commonalities surrounding these issues as they pertain to Africa's 54 countries. This reveals some of the major challenges and opportunities relating to the aforementioned transition.

This chapter is organized as follows. Firstly, a brief overview of the previous industrial revolutions is given, followed by an analysis of Africa in the context of these industrial revolutions. Thereafter, the features of 4IR are discussed with key insights relating to current and future disruptions, as well as potential benefits thereof. The issues surrounding Africa's preparedness for 4IR are then explored, considering the major thematic areas of infrastructure, human capacity development and policy, before a brief overview of ongoing progress in Africa in 4IR is discussed. Finally, a summary of the chapter is presented.

## The Four Industrial Revolutions

Over the past two hundred years, the world has already experienced three industrial revolutions, and we are currently in the initial phase of the fourth. The first three industrial revolutions each took place approximately a hundred years apart. However, the fourth industrial revolution is taking place approximately fifty years after the third industrial revolution (see Figure 11.1). Any industrial revolution brings about significant changes in society, that is, changes in the way we do things, the way we interact, the nature of jobs and so on.

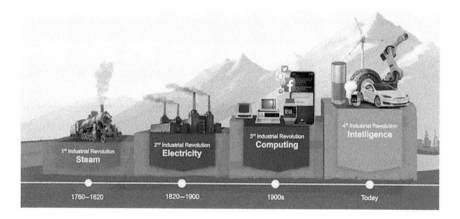

**Figure 11.1** The four industrial revolutions
*Source*: Creative Commons

The first industrial revolution took place in the latter part of the eighteenth century in Great Britain (Allen 2009). The major technological innovation and driving force behind the first industrial revolution was the use of steam power. This led to the mechanization of processes that brought about major developments in agriculture, manufacturing and transportation. Africa was merely a spectator in the first industrial revolution and did not actively participate at the time. Thus, Africa's participation in the first industrial revolution was mostly limited to the extent as determined by colonialists at the time. In fact, the first railway system in Africa was established in Egypt around 50 years after its invention in Great Britain.

The second industrial revolution came about approximately a century after the first. The second industrial revolution was greatly attributed to advancements in science and technology. Electric power and the electric motor, for instance, drastically changed the industrial settings at the time by giving rise to assembly lines in factories, resulting in mass production capability. Significant advancements made in the field of medical sciences aided by better management of diseases led to an increase in the average life expectancy of people. The second industrial revolution was mainly driven by the Western world, and Africa did not actively participate in this revolution, similar to the earlier one.

The third industrial revolution started in the second half of the twentieth century. The electronics industry with the semiconductor transistor made major strides, ushering in the digital age. The advancement of computers also led to automation in industry, thereby vastly improving industrial efficiency, production, and quality. There were also major advances in other sectors like telecommunication. Mobile telephony started during this industrial revolution, becoming more sophisticated over the years, with different generations of mobile communication paving the way for services like data communications along with the basic voice communication.

The fourth industrial revolution occurred approximately half a century after the third industrial revolution. 4IR is not based on a single technology or technological innovation but a confluence of multiple technologies. Some of the technological pillars of the fourth industrial revolution are artificial intelligence (AI), blockchain, Internet of Things (IoT), cyber-physical Systems (CPS), robotics, additive manufacturing and 3D printing, augmented and virtual reality, 5G wireless technology and so on. The technological disruptions brought about by 4IR goes well beyond specific industrial sectors and has begun to permeate every aspect of human existence.

## Africa in the Context of Industrial Revolutions

The origins of modern humans have been traced back to the African continent (Chan et al. 2019). As we take the next leap forward in science and technology in Africa, clearer hindsight reveals not only how the continent has paced slowly behind in recent history (Goodwill 2014), but also the tremendous contributions that indigenous African scientific discovery and technological application have made in the past (Lovejoy 2014). Relatively recently, there has been a greater emphasis on revealing the true nature of Africa's role in science and technology to humankind (Horsthemke 2017). This stems from the growing recognition of postcolonial heritage on the continent and a drive towards gaining a deeper understanding of the richness of African indigenous knowledge and the value that this may bring to light, as Africa moves forward with its postcolonial experiences (Shizha 2016).

Prior to the programming of much of the African continent to adopt the Eurocentric ideas of development, Africa had developed its own technology from its own scientific knowledge (Shizha 2016). This indigenous knowledge comprised not only tremendous insight and experience in agriculture and hunting but also accomplishments in areas as we know them today inter alia mathematics, architecture, astronomy, textile manufacture, mining, metallurgy, navigation and medicine (Blatch 2013). In fact, many archaeological field projects have yielded discoveries of indigenous African technologies that dispute the prior identification of the continent's historical technological inferiority (Killick 2015).

If technological development is regarded as a phenomenon that is directly related to sociocultural context, that is, suitability of technological development is based on the society its serves, then the indigenous knowledge systems of Africa provided tremendous value and deserves recognition (Shizha 2016). Undoubtedly, African indigenous skills and practical knowledge certainly have a role to play and must thus be reclaimed as part of the continent's progress (Horsthemke 2017).

It is with this backdrop that Africa can get a sense of and hone in on its true potential in the fourth industrial revolution. The indigenous African knowledge and technology systems can provide true value in the context of the digital era because there is much to be learned from these past systems; there is value in taking them forward as although there is a postcolonial context, the African societal context is still very much present; our environments have been modified to an extent, but the value of these systems in better understanding our natural resources is still valid; and there is also value in recognizing, reclaiming and reviving these systems (Ezenagu 2014), in order to leapfrog into the fourth industrial revolution – whereby context and sustainable development are key.

The inexorable link between social and technological systems are particularly complex in Africa's history. While there is much to learn about the role of science and technology in Africa during the precolonial era – as previously mentioned – more recent technological and scientific developments in Africa are directly related to the external necessitation of colonial times. As such, Africa was never seen to be at the frontier of science and technology, particularly over the periods of the previous industrial revolutions, and it inherited a pattern of dependency on external partners for technological development (Austen 1983). However, Africa has managed to leapfrog over the European, Asian and American technological steps in certain instances. There are fundamental differences between these past and current circumstances, in that, Africa faces the latest industrial revolution under very different social and political circumstances and the technological developments of the day are more easily adopted and adapted to open up pathways to the global village.

## Preparedness of Africa for the Fourth Industrial Revolution

As already described, developments in 4IR are occurring at an incredible rate, and the African continent needs to proactively respond in a strategic and sustainable manner. There are vast opportunities and benefits that Africa could potentially draw from 4IR, noting that there is also the daunting prospect of further inequality resulting from an inadequate response to 4IR. These particular issues are dealt with in greater detail later on in the chapter. Before analyzing the potential of 4IR in Africa, we first investigate Africa's state of readiness – or preparedness – for 4IR. In taking a whole-of-Africa approach here, it is not practicable to suggest that this investigation into preparedness provides sufficient detail for an entire continent as vast and diverse as Africa with a population of approximately 1.2 billion spanning over 54 countries. Thus, a high-level approach is adopted through considering particularly representative instances in the context of broad thematic areas – that is, infrastructure, human capacity and policy, as shown in Figure 11.2. These have found to be key elements or success criteria for placing African economies on a sustainable growth path in 4IR (Das et al. 2020).

The World Economic Forum (WEF) has established the global competitive index 4.0, or GCI 4.0, which benchmarks countries and regions according to 12 pillars – that is, institutions, infrastructure, ICT adoption, macroeconomic stability, health, skills, product market, labour market, financial system, market size, business dynamism and innovation capability (Schwab 2019). A summary of the rankings and scores for African countries as listed in the report is given in Table 11.1.

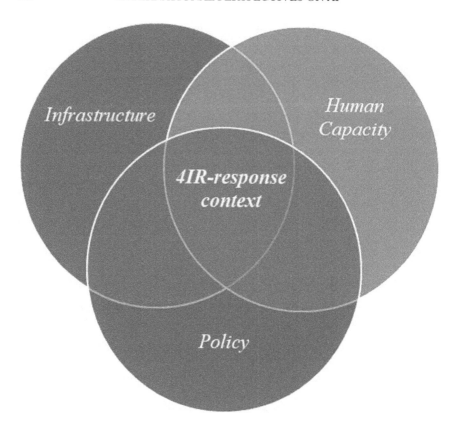

**Figure 11.2** High-level approach to investigating Africa's 4IR preparedness/readiness with respect to key thematic areas
*Source*: Author's own

### Infrastructure

In general, Africa suffers from an infrastructure deficit, but this is less of a challenge in 4IR because there many of the relevant technologies that do not require the legacy of extensive systems and processes (Smith 2019). An exemplar is the telecommunications boom in Africa. Many regions did not have existing legacy telecommunications infrastructure before the mobile telecommunications boom on the continent. Mobile technology has been a revelation to Africa's information and communication technology (ICT) infrastructure deficit. In fact, many doubted any future prospects of telecommunications becoming a widespread public service in Africa, and yet modern ICTs in the form of mobile phones, internet and computers have become a major part of progress and development on the continent (Njoh

**Table 11.1** Summary of African countries according to 2019 WEF Global Competitive Index 4.0

| African Country | Ranking (out of 141 countries globally) | Score (Highest:84.8, Lowest: 35.1) |
|---|---|---|
| Mauritius | 52 | 64.3 |
| South Africa | 60 | 62.4 |
| Morocco | 75 | 60.0 |
| Seychelles | 76 | 56.6 |
| Tunisia | 87 | 56.4 |
| Algeria | 89 | 56.3 |
| Botswana | 91 | 55.5 |
| Egypt | 93 | 54.5 |
| Namibia | 94 | 54.5 |
| Kenya | 95 | 54.1 |
| Rwanda | 100 | 52.8 |
| Ghana | 111 | 51.2 |
| Cape Verde | 112 | 50.8 |
| Senegal | 114 | 49.7 |
| Uganda | 115 | 48.9 |
| Nigeria | 116 | 48.3 |
| Tanzania | 117 | 48.2 |
| Côte d'Ivoire | 118 | 48.1 |
| Gabon | 119 | 47.5 |
| Zambia | 120 | 46.5 |
| Eswatini | 121 | 46.4 |
| Guinea | 122 | 46.1 |
| Cameroon | 123 | 46.0 |
| Gambia, The | 124 | 45.9 |
| Benin | 125 | 45.8 |
| Ethiopia | 126 | 44.4 |
| Zimbabwe | 127 | 44.2 |
| Malawi | 128 | 43.7 |
| Mali | 129 | 43.6 |
| Burkina Faso | 130 | 43.4 |
| Lesotho | 131 | 42.9 |
| Madagascar | 132 | 42.9 |
| Mauritania | 134 | 40.9 |
| Burundi | 135 | 40.3 |
| Angola | 136 | 38.1 |
| Mozambique | 137 | 38.1 |
| Democratic Republic of Congo. | 139 | 36.1 |
| Chad | 141 | 35.1 |

*Source:* Schwab (2019).

2018). Albeit that this industrial revolution does not strictly require the legacy of extensive systems and processes, there is still some fundamental infrastructure needed to engage and seize opportunities in 4IR.

An example of the movement away from traditional infrastructure required for actively participating in previous industrial revolutions is in the energy sector. There is now a shift away from large-scale centralized systems that require extensive infrastructure to more distributed systems – utilizing renewable energy sources – situated closer to the consumer. Similarly, as with the case of the telecommunications, the large-scale infrastructure of the past era is not a prerequisite for adopting decentralized renewable energy systems. Furthermore, the African continent is blessed with an abundance of renewable energy sources including hydro, wind, solar and biomass. The associated technological infrastructure is also readily available, flexible, scalable and reliable. Many African countries even have ample resources to adopt and modify – including locally sourced and manufactured components – to put in place the necessary energy infrastructure. There have been several efforts and initiatives underway in this regard on the African continent. An example of this is the Africa Renewable Energy Initiative (AREI), led by the African Union and supported by African Heads of State and Government on Climate Change (CAHOSCC), which is aimed at harnessing Africa's renewable energy potential to establish 300 GW generation capacity by 2030 (AREI 2018). New Partnership for Africa's Development (NEPAD) has been leading similar programmes in recent years, such as Renewable Energy Access Programme (REAP), and has identified that some of the key challenges, among others, with developing and implementing these projects are lack of development capacity, inadequate expertise in the public sector and unfavourable investment environments (PIDA 2020).

Some studies have benchmarked infrastructure with respect to ICT and 4IR preparedness. One such study is the Global Connectivity Index (GCI) – completed by Huawei – that ranks countries annually according to their ICT investment and maturity, and their digital economic performance (Hauwei, 2019). According to the GCI 2019, with respect to the African countries out of 79 ranked countries, South Africa appears in the "Adopters" category and Egypt, Morocco, Algeria, Botswana, Ghana, Kenya, Namibia, Nigeria, Tanzania, Uganda and Ethiopia appear in the "Starters" category. A summary of the African countries' ranking is given in Table 11.2, noting that the highest score is 85 and the lowest is 23. It should also be highlighted that there is an expectedly high correlation between GDPs and GCI scores of countries.

According to the aforementioned WEF GCI 4.0, for the infrastructure and ICT adoption pillars, out of the seven regions benchmarked in 2019, sub-Saharan Africa scored the lowest, while North Africa performed better than Latin America and the Caribbean, and South Asia (Schwab 2019).

**Table 11.2** Summary of African countries according to 2019 Global Competitive Index

| African Country | Rank (out of 79 globally) | Score (Highest – 85, Lowest – 23) |
|---|---|---|
| South Africa | 52 | 43 |
| Egypt | 58 | 37 |
| Morocco | 61 | 36 |
| Algeria | 68 | 31 |
| Botswana | 70 | 30 |
| Ghana | 71 | 29 |
| Kenya | 72 | 29 |
| Namibia | 74 | 28 |
| Nigeria | 75 | 27 |
| Tanzania | 77 | 24 |
| Uganda | 78 | 24 |
| Ethiopia | 79 | 23 |

*Source:* Huawei (2019).

With the rise of IoT, cloud computing and AI, data centres have become essential building blocks of a modern economy. In order to become more self-sufficient, provide adequate processing capabilities for industries, and protect national data resources, African countries will need their own data centres. Various sectors of the economy such as agriculture, healthcare, transport, mining, financial services and more thrive on innovating through data resources. Employing 4IR technologies such as cloud computing and AI requires investment in the provision of modern data centre services that have become the feature of a modern state. Finally, the provision of last-mile connectivity is an essential one in 4IR. Although much of the African continent faces a deficit in fixed infrastructure, there is tremendous opportunity for the uptake of mobile systems infrastructure – as the mobile telecommunications boom has shown us. Thus, 5G technologies' infrastructure must be aggressively pursued in Africa for deployment in far-flung areas around the continent, whereby sparsely populated regions can gain access and support for their local economies.

### Human Capacity

As with any of the previous industrial revolutions, the way we live, interact and work are changing rapidly in 4IR. For any economy to thrive in 4IR, a skilled and capable workforce is essential. Thus, the ability of Africa and its nations to develop and mobilize the necessary human capacity is of utmost importance.

According to the WEF report on the future of jobs (WEF 2016), studies show that the top skills required in 2020 are, inter alia, complex problem solving, critical thinking, creativity and cognitive flexibility. The importance of cognitive flexibility is extremely valuable in 4IR whereby technology is rapidly changing and norms are being disrupted, and hence the adaptability of the workforce becomes a crucial success factor. The report also points out that in-demand tech-based skills in areas such as AI and machine learning are in deficit and is already impacting industries.

Africa has a huge human capital potential through its youth and female populations. The continent does have the youngest population and is expected to have approximately 42 per cent of the world's youth by 2030 (Perlotto 2019). A youthful population, together with a female population of greater than half the total population, gives Africa the opportunity to seize untapped energetic human capital to bolster its progress in 4IR. In 4IR, the nature of work has also changed with more flexibility and different types of work, which opens new opportunities for youth and women.

Thus, African nations have the twofold task in terms of human capacity development – that is, a focus on the development of new programmes and initiatives for preparing their youth for the future and also to rapidly upskill and reskill their current labour forces. In 2015, the Africa-America Institute (AAI) published a report on the state of education in Africa, which revealed some key findings in terms of the different areas of human capacity development that are quite relevant to the discussion around Africa in 4IR (AAI 2015). Selected key findings with particular areas of concern are as follows (AAI 2015):

- Early childhood education: Most African countries have very few pre-primary school programs that enable children to reach their development potential. This is crucial for school readiness and improves outcomes of primary school education.
- Secondary education: There are still a large number of adolescents who must travel long distances to attend secondary schools and/or drop out to start work. This has a tremendous impact on the success rates of secondary schools across Africa.
- Technical and vocational education and training (TVET): Majority of African countries are not focused on TVET. Much more investment is required in this area of capacity development.
- Tertiary education: Sub-Saharan Africa has especially low rates of enrolments. Further expanding of access to university programmes is needed.

- Investment in education: While public investment in education in Africa is generally higher (as a percentage of GDP) than most countries globally, there needs to be more public-private partnerships to improve investments in education systems.
- Quality of education and building a suitably skilled workforce: There must be a concerted effort by governments to ensure the availability of suitably trained teachers and instructors. Additionally, Africa does suffer from a shortage of highly skilled African talent, which means a review and appropriate reform of curricula is necessary.

In the era of 4IR, there are key enablers in terms of human capacity development – besides the aforementioned – that African countries should take on board, which are embracing digital fluency and literacy as well as life-long learning at all levels of education; more flexible and accessible professional development programmes leading to key competencies and skills development; investment in local research and development in areas of 4IR; creating entrepreneurship skills and culture of innovation.

## *Policy*

Before gaining independence, African countries were mostly geared towards production, infrastructure and logistics largely concerned with the export of raw commodities (Diop 2015). According to Diop, this was the case with most systems in Africa, which were largely concerned with the colonial endeavours. For example, education systems were not directed towards endowing Africans with training and skills to transform African economies but rather to cater to colonial structures. And while African countries began gaining independence in the 1960s and while there were policy reforms, these have not been providing any significant transformation, with economies still largely dependent on unimproved commodities (Diop 2015). But in recent times, there has been some sustained economic growth, enhanced policy reforms as many overarching policy frameworks in Africa begin to make strides in infrastructure investment, improved production, and improved public services.

The human development index (HDI) is a key compound measure provided by the United Nations (UN) for assessing human development in countries, which comprises life expectancy (including health and well-being), education and living standards. In 2019, out of 189 countries indexed globally, 5 African countries rank in the top 100, 9 African countries are ranked at a very high or high HDI, 11 are rated at medium HDI, with the rest of Africa at a low HDI (Conceição 2019). Although these are a seemingly poor reflection of human development in Africa, it should be highlighted that there has been a significant and sustained improvement across Africa, with most countries improving their HDI values in recent years.

In relation to the aforementioned lack of transition of African economies into export of improved commodities, there is also a need for significant improvement of high technology exports. Africa has far less than the world average in terms of this measure, meaning that most African counties are importers of high technology rather than exporters (World Bank 2020). In 4IR, the ability to locally innovate is essential towards achieving sustained economic growth. Thus, African policy-makers have to firmly fix their attention on incentivizing local innovation, developing science and technology capacity – including training more researchers and creating a fertile environment for technopreneurship.

As previously highlighted, the establishment of national data centres in Africa is necessary for securing and extracting value from national data resources. Accompanying policy and legislation are crucial to ensuring that Africa can benefit from its data in a sustainable and ethical manner that is cohesive with its strategic intents as well as that of the UN's sustainable development goals. This includes provision for not only enhancing the development and security of local technological resources but also promoting ethics around development and application. Finally, policy frameworks surrounding the pan-African agenda will be key in 4IR for, inter alia, improving transfer and exchange of technological and intellectual resources, enabling financial flows and borderless human capacity development programmes.

## Ongoing Progress in Africa in the Era of 4IR

Countries have already begun formulating and implementing policies and strategies around the world as early as 2016–17 (FoLI 2020). Some countries in Africa have also proactively begun developing their own strategies, gathering resources and putting forward legislation to support their efforts to reap the benefits of 4IR. In 2018, Kenya established an AI and blockchain taskforce to investigate and recommend how the country can leverage these technologies. In the same year, Tunisia also began developing a national AI strategy. South Africa established the Presidential Commission of the Fourth Industrial Revolution in 2019, to develop a strategy so that the country can effectively participate in the revolution (DTPS 2019). In 2019, Egypt developed its national AI strategy, focusing on capacity building and application of the technology (OECDAI 2020). Morocco has also created an extensive digital transformation agenda (Lou et al. 2019). Rwanda has also reviewed and renewed its industrial policy to intensify structural reform and align itself towards opportunities in 4IR (Shepherd and Twum 2018). There have been several engagements and forums held across Africa in various countries around developing strategies and plans for 4IR. It should be highlighted here that there are several promising developments, projects, initiatives and activities in many countries across Africa. Some of these are presented as cases studies in a recent report by the African Development Bank (AfDB 2019).

## Conclusion

The African continent is vast and diverse, with over 1.2 billion people across 54 countries. It is thus expected that the proclivity – let alone preparedness – for 4IR will vary across Africa. Moreover, the anticipated benefits or opportunities will similarly differ. Thus, the strategic adoption of 4IR technologies and capabilities must be firmly rooted in the context of the region and the country. That being said, 4IR is unlike any other industrial revolution, in that, there is the flexibility to adopt and adapt platforms that can best suit strengths and weaknesses to ultimately set sustainable growth paths for economies and improve lives of citizens. Generally, infrastructure is essential for active engagement in an industrial revolution, but in 4IR much of legacy systems and processes are not strict prerequisites for gaining access to the potential benefits. This means that Africa does not require certain infrastructure including some ICT and energy systems, as more recent advancements in technology enable flexible, scalable and cost-effective means of putting in place necessary infrastructure without the need to have in place any legacy systems. This makes leapfrogging possible with respect to certain infrastructure for 4IR as discussed in this chapter. Another critical component of reflection in the age of 4IR is human capacity. Here, we find that Africa has tremendous opportunity presented by its youthful and relatively high female populations to not only give energy towards realizing its 4IR ambitions but also promote equality and accessibility to its economy. The work presented in this chapter also found that while there is much to be done in terms of human development in Africa, most countries have shown sustained improvement in this regard, reflecting Africa's efforts in policy reforms. Sustainable growth trajectories in 4IR also implore additional policy and legislative measures particularly in relation to infrastructure investment, incentivizing local innovation, development of science and technology capacity, creating a supportive environment for technopreneurship, enhancing development and security of local technological resources, promotion of ethical technology development and application that is aligned with the SDGs, as well as the promotion of the pan-African agenda facilitating technological and intellectual resource transfer and exchange, financial flows and borderless human capacity development. Some highlights of critical initiatives across the continent demonstrate the positivity and pro-activeness of African nations to pursue the opportunities offered by 4IR. However, a more aggressive and coherent approach across Africa – with specific consideration of the issues highlighted in this chapter – will be most advantageous for the continent and its people.

## References

Africa-America Institute (AAI). 2015. State of education in Africa report, 2015: A report card on the progress, opportunities and challenges confronting the African education sector. https://greatsocieties.com/AAI-2015.pdf.

African Development Bank (AfDB). 2019. *Potential of the Fourth Industrial Revolution in Africa.* Study Report: Unlocking the potential of the fourth industrial revolution in Africa.

Africa Renewable Energy Initiative (AREI). 2015. A framework for transforming Africa towards a renewable energy powered future with access for all. http://www.arei.org/wp-content/uploads/2018/09/AREI-Framework.pdf.

Allen, Robert C. 2009. *The British Industrial Revolution in Global Perspective.* Cambridge: Cambridge University Press.

Austen, Ralph A., and Daniel Headrick. (1983). The role of technology in the African past. *African Studies Review*, 26(3/4): 163–84.

Blatch, Sydella. 2013. Great achievements in science and technology in ancient Africa. *ASBMB Today.* https://www.asbmb.org/asbmb-today/science/020113/great-achievements-in-stem-in-ancient-africa.

Bright, J. 2016. A brief overview of Africa's tech industry – and 7 predictions for its future. World Economic Forum. https://www.weforum.org/agenda/2016/05/a-brief-history-of-africa-s-tech-industry-and-7-predictions-for-its-future/.

Chan, E. K., A. Timmermann, B. F. Baldi, A. E. Moore, R. J. Lyons, S. S. Lee, A. M. Kalsbeek, D. C. Petersen, H. Rautenbach, H. E. Förtsch and M. R. Bornman. 2019. Human origins in a Southern African Palaeo-Wetland and first migrations. *Nature*, 575(7781): 185–89.

Conceição, P., 2019. Human development report 2019: Beyond income, beyond averages, beyond today: Inequalities in human development in the 21st century. United Nations Development Programme. http://hdr.undp.org/sites/default/files/hdr2019.pdf.

Das, G. G., and I. Drine. 2020. Distance from the technology frontier: How could Africa catch-up via socio-institutional factors and human capital? *Technological Forecasting and Social Change*, 150: 119755. https://www.sciencedirect.com/science/article/pii/S0040162517301968.

Department of Telecommunications and Postal Services (DTPS). 2019. Terms of Reference for the Presidential Commission on the Fourth Industrial Revolution. Government Gazette General Notices Notice 209 of 2019. South African Government April 2019.

Diop, M. (2015). Policymaking in Africa: Reflections from decades of experience. The World Bank. https://www.worldbank.org/en/news/speech/2015/03/31/policymaking-in-africa-reflections-from-decades-of-experience.

Ezenagu, Ngozi. (2014). The blight of African indigenous technology in the 21st century: The way forward. *Journal of Tourism and Heritage Studies*, 3(1): 59–73.

Future of Life Institute (FoLI). 2020. National and international AI strategies. https://futureoflife.org/national-international-ai-strategies/.

Godwill, E. A., 2014. Science and technology in Africa: the key elements and measures for sustainable development. *Global Journal of Science Frontier Research: G Bio-tech and Genetics*, 14(2): 17–28.

Horsthemke, K., 2017. Indigenous (African) knowledge systems, science, and technology. In Adeshina Afolayan and Toyin Falola (eds.), *The Palgrave Handbook of African Philosophy*, pp, 585–603. New York: Palgrave Macmillan.

Huawei. 2019. Powering intelligent connectivity with global collaboration: Mapping your transformation into a digital economy with GCI 2019. Global Connectivity Index. https://www.huawei.com/minisite/gci/assets/files/gci_2019_whitepaper_en.pdf?v=20191217v2.

Killick, David. (2015). Invention and innovation in African iron-smelting technologies. *Cambridge Archaeological Journal*, 25(1): 307.

Lou, K. K., F. Sadeski and M. Lacave. 2019. Study on unlocking the potential of the fourth industrial revolution in Africa, Country case: Morocco. Technopolis group. https://4irpotential.africa/wp-content/uploads/2019/10/Morocco-Case-study-Temp.pdf.

Lovejoy, Paul E. 2014. African contributions to science, technology and development. *UNESCO: The Slave Route Project. Collective Volume.* 1–38. http://www.unesco.org/new/fileadmin/MULTIMEDIA/HQ/CLT/pdf/P_Lovejoy_African_Contributions_Eng_01.pdf.

Marwala, T. 2019. Preparing Africa for the fourth industrial revolution. World Intellectual Property Organisation (WIPO) Magazine. https://www.wipo.int/wipo_magazine/en/2019/si/article_0006.html.

Mead, D. 2017. Here's how Africa can take advantage of the fourth industrial revolution. World Economic Forum. https://www.weforum.org/agenda/2017/05/heres-how-africa-can-take-advantage-of-the-fourth-industrial-revolution/.

Ndung'u, N. S., and L. Signé. 2020. Capturing the fourth industrial revolution: A regional and national agenda. Foresight Africa 2020 report, ch 5.

Njoh, A. J. 2018. The relationship between modern information and communications technologies (ICTs) and development in Africa. *Utilities Policy*, 50: 83–90. https://www.sciencedirect.com/science/article/pii/S0957178717301157.

OECD AI Policy Observatory. 2020. Egypt's AI strategy. https://oecd.ai/dashboards/policy-initiatives/2019-data-policyInitiatives-26476.

Perlotto, S. 2019. Africa's future: Youth and the data defining their lives. Population Reference Bureau. https://www.prb.org/africas-future-youth-and-the-data-defining-their-lives/.

Programme for Infrastructure Development in Africa (PIDA). 2020. Renewable Energy Access Programme (REAP). https://www.au-pida.org/renewable-energy-access-programme-reap/.

Radu, S. 2020. Africa braces for the fourth industrial revolution. US News & World report. https://www.usnews.com/news/best-countries/articles/2020-01-23/the-stakes-for-africa-in-the-fourth-industrial-revolution.

Schwab, K. ed. 2019. The global competitiveness report 2019. World Economic Forum. http://www3.weforum.org/docs/WEF_TheGlobalCompetitivenessReport2019.pdf.

Shepherd, B., and A. Twum. 2018. Review of industrial policy in Rwanda: Data review, comparative assessment, and discussion points. International Growth Centre, F-38426-RWA-1. https://www.theigc.org/wp-content/uploads/2018/11/Shepherd-Twum-2018-Final-report.pdf.

Shizha, E., 2016. African indigenous perspectives on technology. In Gloria Emeagwali and Edward Shizha (eds.), *African Indigenous Knowledge and the Sciences*, pp. 47–62. Rotterdam: Sense Publishers.

Smith C. 2019. Revolutionary technologies will drive African prosperity – this is why. World Economic Forum. https://www.weforum.org/agenda/2019/09/why-the-4ir-is-a-fast-track-to-african-prosperity/.

World Bank, World Development Indicators. (2020). High technology exports [Data file]. https://data.worldbank.org/indicator/TX.VAL.TECH.MF.ZS.

World Economic Forum (WEF). 2016. The future of jobs: Employment, skills and work-force strategy for the fourth industrial revolution. In Global challenge insight report. Geneva: World Economic Forum.

# Chapter 12

# THE ADOPTION OF ARTIFICIAL INTELLIGENCE WITHIN THE CARIBBEAN: RESUSCITATING THE CARICOM'S SINGLE MARKET AND ECONOMY

## Kai-Ann D. Skeete

## Introduction

Since time immemorial, the small island states of the Caribbean have continuously developed regional integration schemes to achieve greater independence and development among themselves. This has resulted in several multipronged approaches to integration covering a wide scope. The Caribbean Community and Common Market (CARICOM) was established by the Treaty of Chaguaramas, which was signed by Barbados, Guyana, Jamaica and Trinidad and Tobago and came into effect on 1 August 1973, after which 11 other territories joined.

CARICOM is a unique arrangement. According to Payne (1994), writing in the second decade of its existence, CARICOM's survival was secured on the basis that it would steer clear of Caribbean political integration and all its facets, namely supranationalism, which threatens national independence and sovereignty. With respect to its governance mechanisms, Payne's discussion describes the CARICOM system as being managed by a chain of organs comprised of member states' politicians and is merely 'serviced by its secretariat'. Decision-making within the Community has to be by unanimous agreement but the implementation of all decisions is up to the individual member state and 'its own constitutional procedures' (1994).

In following the trends of regional integration worldwide, the European Union has launched its AI strategy and roadmap. However, in the conceptualization of AI within the Caribbean, the author affirms the belief that as developed countries increase their adoption of AI, the gap between the developing and developed countries will widen (Szcepanski 2019).

This research aims to examine the utilization of artificial intelligence (AI) within the Caribbean. This topic was selected with the aim of identifying key trends in AI within CARICOM. An assessment of key private sectors, regional organizations and civil society representatives across four CARICOM territories as well as national policymakers involved in the information and communication technology (ICT) arena was done to identify related opportunities in AI within CARICOM and the subsequent prospects for increasing economic growth, ethical governance and cross-border flows.

## Introduction of the CARICOM Single Market and Economy (CSME)

As with previous integration attempts, upon realizing the limitations of the regional initiative, Caribbean heads of governments agreed to deepen their state of regional integration and thus conceptualized a Caribbean Single Market and Economy. Twenty-seven years after the start the of the Regional Independence movement, CARICOM heads of governments, at the 10th Meeting of the Conference at Grand Anse, Grenada, in 1989, agreed to deepen the integration process by conceptualising a regional single market and economy. This was to be achieved 'in the shortest possible time' with the hope of strengthening the regional community to respond to the challenges and opportunities posed by the changing neoliberal international environment.

Thus, former prime minister of Barbados aptly described the CSME as the 'unique and strategic tool for CARICOM whilst we attempt to reposition our economies to compete effectively in a globalising world'(Arthur 2004). Hence, it was envisaged that the CSME would assist CARICOM in achieving its goals ranging from improving national standards of living, increasing levels of employment and achieving comprehensive development.

## CARICOM Single ICT Space

The CARICOM Single ICT Space was first introduced as a pivotal recommendation for the Regional Digital Development Strategy, which was created with an aim of improving ICT within the Caribbean region. Essentially, it was conceptualized as the 'digital layer' of the CSME, which is considered to be a 'cross-sectoral and highly complex undertaking' (Secretariat 2017; Secretariat 2018). It allows for the regional harmonization of all ICT and legislative framework as well as the removal of cellular roaming charges within the region (Secretariat 2018).

According to the deputy programme manager, ICT for Development at CARICOM, Jennifer Britton, the CARICOM Single ICT Space is

> envisioned as an ICT enabled borderless space that fosters economic, social and cultural integration for the betterment of Caribbean citizens. (CTU 2017)

> Thus ensuring that the Caribbean citizenry is comprised of digital entrepreneurs, digital citizens and digital problem-solvers. (Marius 2019)

Caribbean FutureScape writes about the possibilities that the Single ICT Space can offer such as a unique regional digital identification card that would grant citizens a more integrated, productive and efficient Caribbean as users would be "able to access local and regional government services such as business registration, hospital records as well as the ability to purchase goods and real estate using digital currency" (CTU 2019).

## AI within CARICOM

AI has grown and developed significantly over the past decade, and the use of AI is key to the successful progression of the CARICOM Single ICT Space. Brathwaite describes AI as comprising either machines and systems that acquire and apply knowledge while executing intelligent behavior, or the use of software-based operations like Siri and Alexa in the virtual world (Brathwaite 2019). Amazon's Alexa, Google Translate, smart cities and houses, driverless cars all illustrate that a new dawn is here to stay (Hajela 2016). Simply put, Thierer et al. state, AI is 'an umbrella term for technologies that appear to act as if they were rational beings' (Thierer et al. 2017).

One of the main catalysts behind the implementation of AI technology is 'primarily economic' (Scott and Lorenz 2018). The Jamaican minister of technology is on record as stating that approximately '30% of all day-to-day businesses will implement AI as part of their digital transformation strategy' (Gleaner 2019). Therefore, one would expect that that there may be an increase in unemployment while on the path to successfully achieve efficiency and effectiveness (Fay 2019). This researcher is hoping that the adoption and implementation of AI within the Caribbean will be human-centric and complementary to current processes.

## Challenges of AI within the Caribbean

The G20 recognized that due to AI there will be challenges within the society and the cyber community, and the labour market with respect to 'privacy, security, ethical issues, new digital divides and the need for AI capacity building' (Group-20 2019). The main challenge to the adoption and utilization of AI within the Caribbean surrounds the limited availability of data. AI requires big data in the form of datasets to generate predictions and patterns. 'These datasets are so massive and complex, that traditional data-processing application software is inadequate to deal with them' (Deyal 2018).

## Opportunities for AI within the Caribbean

Scott and Lorenz make the point that countries 'cannot shape the future of AI without first choosing objectives and paths toward them' (Scott and Lorenz 2018). This author identifies a few sectors where AI should be adopted and implemented within the Caribbean.

### Demographic Data

Policymakers could seek to capture the big data from the satellites, technological devices and social media as a means of 'replac(ing) traditional methods of acquiring socioeconomic data' (Cohen and Kharas 2018).

### Weather/Natural Disasters

Within the Caribbean, we spend six months of the year from June to November on the lookout for hurricanes and other devastating impacts of climate change such as flooding. The deployment of AI gives the government the ability to 'predict and monitor natural disasters' (Joshi 2019).

### Agriculture

Agriculture is one of the more important sectors to the Caribbean as it struggles to achieve food security. Deyal advances that through the use of AI applications, farmers would be given more accurate data 'to predict the ideal types and amounts of fertilizer, soil water and other variables for the best crop growth' (Deyal 2018).

### Trade

Meltzer argues that AI can 'have a transformative impact on international trade' (2018). This is as a result of the development and utilization of translation services on digital platforms. To further support this claim, the Eastern Caribbean States have introduced the utilization of AI within negotiation theatres/platforms to provide resources to read and analyse text quickly. The following example illustrates this:

A recent test confirmed the ability of the platform to review 5 pages of a trade agreement in 26 seconds while the usual time taken to undertake an analysis of the same documents by lawyers approximately 92 minutes. (Campbell 2018)

## *Healthcare*

As the governments of SIDS are often stretched to provide adequate resources to take care of the health of the wider population, AI could be used 'providing virtual nurses which are capable of monitoring patients at a lower cost' (Deyal 2018). In addition, artificial neural networks assist in the diagnosing of medical conditions as well as indicating the correct treatment (Thierer et al. 2017).

## Survey Analysis and Discussion of Findings

The author administered an online 18-point survey item to national, regional and civil society ICT practitioners in four CARICOM member states (Barbados, Grenada, Jamaica and St. Lucia). Out of 20 surveys, 13 were returned representing a 65 per cent response rate. Although all of the surveyed practitioners have some knowledge of AI, only the lone female civil society respondent based in Barbados utilizes AI within her day-to-day operations at work.

The Caribbean Single ICT Space was launched in 2017 and there are ICT professionals within the 14 independent CARICOM territories; only a small fraction of respondents (15 per cent) indicated an awareness of the Caribbean Single ICT Space, which is a concern for a future Caribbean that wishes to adopt AI.

A key component to introducing AI within the Caribbean is determining the level of comfort people have using AI. Thirty-five per cent of the respondents are comfortable with AI automated systems, 17 per cent are comfortable with AI customer service systems, 15 per cent are comfortable with AI financial services, 15 per cent are comfortable with AI home security, followed by 12 per cent who are comfortable with AI in the construction sector. A mere 3 per cent of the respondents were comfortable with AI conducting surgical procedures and 3 per cent with AI-driven transportation within the Caribbean.

In response to the question asking whether AI impacts the respondents' work, 69 per cent respondents indicated that it impacts none of their work. AI impacts some of the work for 23 per cent of the respondents, while 7 per cent stated that AI impacts all of the work they do. Respondents in the commercial banking sector, regional security, agriculture and civil society organizations indicated in the affirmative that AI impacts their work.

In response to the question asking whether their organization has plans of implementing AI, more than half of the respondents indicated that the organization had no such plans. While 38 per cent of respondents indicated that their organization had plans to implement AI in the future, only one respondent, representing a commercial banking institution in Jamaica, indicated that their organization was in the process of implementing AI. It is unfortunate that none of the regional respondents were using AI in mission-central operations.

The respondents were asked to select a list of AI tools that were implemented within their organization during the previous six months. The majority of the respondents indicated that workplace collaboration tools/applications, mobile technology or other network-based tools, cloud-based data storage and management tools, and non-cloud-based data storage, management or analysis tools were implemented at varying levels over the previous six months.

Participants were asked the following question: 'In your organization, which of the following operational areas have the greatest opportunities for AI tool implementation?' In response, 76 per cent of the respondents indicated cybersecurity, followed by 69 per cent who indicated data analytics/science, followed by 30 per cent indicating AI tools for customer service/citizen evaluation followed by 23 per cent for program delivery. Incidentally, the lowest levels of affirmative responses were 15 per cent in support of using AI tools for staffing/human capital management and another 15 per cent for acquisition/procurement of tools.

In response to the organizational barriers within the four CARICOM member states as it relates to AI implementation, 92 per cent indicated budget/financial constraints followed by 53 per cent selecting organizational roadblocks; 53 per cent stated a lack of conceptual understanding and 46 per cent lack of technical expertise

Respondents were asked about the potential of AI to disrupt their respective industries. Three respondents indicated that it should make their respective industries more efficient, while one respondent did not think that AI would disrupt their industry soon.

Respondents were asked what were the main issues and challenges affecting their organizations' implementation of an AI regime. The following represents the responses submitted:

- 'The organization is stuck in bureaucracy'
- 'Understanding of AI and recognition that AI can improve the efficiency of the organization'.
- 'My organization has invested heavily in other technology aids, from which they are still expecting a return on investment. Justifying additional

spend on AI or any other technology would be difficult. There is a level of mistrust which leads senior management to intervene/micro-manage rather than trust the technology that is already in place. Once this is a factor, AI implementation will be impossible. We need buy-in from senior management'.

- 'I think it may be foresight and vision by leadership and technical expertise'.
- 'Not enough funding'.
- 'Lack of understanding the opportunities it presents. Financial constraints. Archaic ideology – continuing to do things the same way even with techno-logical solutions available to improve processes'.
- 'Affordability'.
- 'No scope exists currently'.
- 'Cost (which is a factor of priority). Lack of expertise within the organiza-tion. Not a part of the current five-year strateg.'.
- 'Job losses'.

## CARICOM's Way Forward

One of the biggest challenges with the introduction and widespread use of AI within the CARICOM region is the availability of data, and the regulation and governance of this data. With only a handful of member states having open information systems, and even fewer having data pro-tection regulations, the quest is for CARICOM to set the tone and pave the way for the introduction, adoption and harmonization of AI across the region.

Bennett recommends that Jamaica should consider creating the position of minister of Artificial Intelligence (AI) similar to the United Arab Emirates. The role of the Jamaican minister of AI would be to,

> understand how these smart applications work, and understand the implications of automation/AI, and perform actions like pushing for facilities like Machine Learning Jamaica Institute to exist. (Bennett 2019)

According to Joshi, governments need to develop a roadmap to assist with the simplification of the adoption of AI. They should

> hire experienced researchers and tech experts who have worked with AI; collect good quality data for training the AI-powered application; enlist skilled professionals that can help in creating adoption strategies; Update current in the government organization; Educate government personnel about artificial intelligence. (Joshi 2019)

First, policymakers within the Caribbean generally tend to be 'risk-averse' and conservative. It is recommended that the region consider all the risks and concerns in a rational and productive manner (Thierer et al. 2017).

Second, CARICOM should develop a Common Regional Privacy Principles document to clearly outline the protection of data as well as developing the regulatory environment around AI within key sectors such as national security, transportation and healthcare. It is recommended that the region consider adopting the EU's 'precautionary principle' approach to first ensure that the adoption of AI '.will not cause any harms to individuals, groups, specific entities, cultural norms, or various existing laws or traditions' (Thierer et al. 2017).

Third, the region has to increase its collection and compilation of available data to create large datasets needed for AI. Following this, AI tools should be gradually introduced to all employees across the member states to 'understand and distinguish the myriad of applications of AI technologies so that they are well equipped to appropriately address each kind' (Thierer et al. 2017).

## Conclusion

In conclusion, the Grenadian prime minister Mitchell emphasized that technology can propel the Caribbean in the right direction but stated that collaboration is needed to take advantage of the opportunities provided by the Single ICT Space, which can lead and help with individual (country) development (CTU 2019). The Single ICT Space would be augmented with a well-developed roadmap and regional policy on AI in specific sectors. Together, this can ameliorate several implementation deficits and regional challenges due to the lack of available and frequent data to assist in completing and harmonizing regional decisions.

## References

Arthur, Owen. 2004. The Caribbean single market and economy: The way forward. Speech at the the 30th Anniversary Distinguished Lecture of CARICOM. Bridgetown, Barbados, 23 April 2004.

Bennett, Jordan Micah. 2019. Why Jamaica urgently needs a minister of artificial intelligence. *Jamaica Gleaner*, 29 December.

Brathwaite, Chelcee. 2019. My journey south (part 1) … tracing developments on artificial intelligence in Latin America and the Caribbean. *Trading Thoughts*, 4 December: 9.

Campbell, Curlan. 2018. Region lags behind in artificial intelligence. 28 March. Accessed 29 June 2020. https://www.nowgrenada.com/2018/03/region-lags-behind-in-artificial-intelligence.

Caribbean Telecommunications Union (CTU). 2017. Vision and roadmap for a CARICOM Single ICT Space. Georgetown, Guyana.

CARICOM Today. 2019. CTU Launches 'Caribbean Futurescape' in Trinidad and Tobago. 8 May. Accessed 20 July 2019. https://today.caricom.org/2019/05/07/ctu-launches-caribbean-futurescape-in-trinidad-and-tobago/.

Cohen, Jennifer, and Homi Kharas. 2018. Using big data and artificial intelligence to accelerate global development. Brookings Report, the Brookings Institute, Washington DC.

Deyal, Zubin, 2018. Artificial intelligence and the Caribbean: Caribbean Development Trends. Accessed 13 June 2019. https://blogs.iadb.org/caribbean-dev-trends/en/9397/.

Fay, Robert. 2019. The world faces a turning point on data and AI: Will we learn from the financial crisis? Centre for International Governance Innovation, Waterloo, Canada.

Fevrier, Stephen. 2018. New artificial intelligence to help facilitate trade negotiations for small island developing states. *OECS* . 11 October. Accessed 29 June 2020. https://pressroom.oecs.org/new-artificial-intelligence-to-help-facilitate-trade-negotiations-for-small-island-developing-states.

Gleaner, Jamaica. 2019. Let's start to ready talk about artificial intelligence. *Jamaica Gleaner*, 1 July.

Group-20. 2019. G20 ministerial statement on trade and digital economy. 9 June. Accessed 6 June 2020. https://g20-digital.go.jp/asset/pdf/g20_2019_japan_digital_statement.pdf.

Hajela, Shailendra. 2016. Policy and ethical issues related to artificial intelligence. Regional Standardization Forum for Bridging the Standardization Gap. New Delhi.

Inter-America Development Bank (IDB). 2019. IDB study says artificial intelligence can boost Caribbean economies. *Curaçao Chronicle*, 31 August 2018.

Joshi, Naveen. 2019. How AI can and will predict disasters. 15 March 2019. Accessed September 4, 2019. https://www.forbes.com/sites/cognitiveworld/2019/03/15/how-ai-can-and-will-predict-disasters/#6d01c1225be2.

Marius, Michele. 2019. ICTP 073 – Following up on the Caribbean Single ICT Space, with Jennifer Britton of the CARICOM Secretariat. 18 September 2019. Accessed 8 June 2020. http://www.ict-pulse.com/2019/09/ictp-073-caribbean-single-ict-space-jennifer-britton-caricom-secretariat.

Meltzer, Joshua. 2018. The impact of artificial intelligence on international trade. Brookings Report, Brookings Institute, Washington DC.

Payne, Anthony. 1994. *Charting Caribbean Development*. Miami: University of Florida Press.

Scott, Ben, Stefan Heumann and Philippe Lorenz. 2018. *Artificial Intelligence and Foreign Policy*. Berlin: Stiftung Neue Verantworthung.

Secretariat, CARICOM. 2017. Ministers green-light Single ICT Space integrated work plan. CARICOM. 19 May. Accessed 8 June 2020. csme.caricom.org/press-releases/ministers-green-light-single-ict-space-integrated-work-plan.

———. 2018. Single ICT Space, cyber-security for discussion at ICT officials' meeting. 6 June. Accessed 8 June 8 2020. csme.caricom.org/press-releases/single-ict-space-cyber-security-for-discussion-at-ict-officials-meeting.

Szcepanski, Marcin. 2019. Economic impacts of artificial intelligence (AI). European Parliamentary Research Service. 1 July 2019.

Thierer, Adam, Andrea Castillo O'Sullivan and Raymond Russell. 2017. *Artificial Intelligence and Publci Policy*. Meratus Research, Arlington: Mercatus Center at George Mason University.

United Nations Council for Trade and Development (UNCTAD). 2018. Trade negotiations: Next frontier for artificial intelligence.

# Chapter 13

# HAS AUSTRALIA BEEN LATE IN ADDRESSING THE ARTIFICIAL INTELLIGENCE CHALLENGES?

Maria Beamond and Alan Montague

## Introduction

This study focusses on artificial intelligence (AI) and its impact on Australian industry. AI is threatening organizations by disruption at a globally level. The value of AI to the global economy is expected to increase by US$16 trillion by 2030 (GEF 2017). Organizational leaders are focusing on answering questions such as 'where should we target investment, and what kind of capabilities would enable us to perform better?' (PwC 2017, 4). A report from PricewaterhouseCoopers (PwC 2017) has projected that China will have a 26 per cent gain of GDP in 2030, followed by North America with 14.5 per cent. The report projects a total of 70 per cent (or US$10.7 trillion) of AI's global economic impact. The same report suggests that Europe and developed countries in Asia will benefit significantly with a growth of 9–12 per cent in GDP in 2030. Developing countries in Africa, Latin America and Asia may have a modest gain of about 6 per cent. But what about Australia? Has Australia been late in turning to address the AI challenges?

Like most countries, Australia is experiencing a great change in the way work is performed (ACS 2020; Deloitte 2019; Syam and Sharma 2018). Australia has been a laggard in addressing challenges of AI and creating appropriate policies to deal with AI-disruption (Elliott 2019a, 2019b). This is changing as the Australian government has provided a budget of $29.9 million to enhance AI and machine learning (Future of Life 2020). AI policy initiatives for Australia include: AU$1.4 million for PhD scholarships to support emerging Australian researchers in artificial intelligence and machine learning; an AI Technology Roadmap project recognizing barriers and opportunities to build Australian capability; development and assistance for future government policy; and the development of an Australia AI ethics framework (OECD 2020; DISER 2020).

The Australian tech future or digital economy strategy focuses on integrating businesses, government and community aims to maximize potential benefits and opportunities that are possible by advanced digital technology. In addition, the CSIRO Innovation Fund is a AU\$242 million venture capital fund investing in new spin-off companies, existing start-ups and SMEs to foster technological development. The Next Generation Technologies Fund with a AU\$730 million budget aims to promote innovation and is managed by the Defence Science and Technology which is part of Australia's Department of Defence. It is the second largest public-funded R&D organization in Australia (DDST 2020). The Australian Space Agency is currently working to deliver a framework for the Robotics and AI Command and Control Centre in the future. The Australian government is also working to deliver AI and emerging technologies content in the Australian curriculum. Several universities have created their own institutes which include the Applied Artificial Intelligence Institute ($A^2I^2$) at Deakin University, the Australian Institute for Machine Learning from the University of Adelaide, the 3AI Institute at the Australian National University and CSIRO Data 61, or the Centre for Artificial Intelligence from the University of Technology Sydney (OECD 2020).

Although government and universities are creating strategies to maximize the return on investment as emerging technologies permeate Australian enterprises, the Australian government faces other challenges as do countries across the globe. The technological and economic challenges also raise issues with 'privacy, safety, transparency, accountability, control of AI-enabled systems, strong competition among countries and organisations' (Deloitte 2019, 3), and the potential lack of awareness of these AI frameworks within Australian organizations.

From the business perspective, although Australian industries believe that AI is important to the success of organizations, companies are using AI to keep pace with the competition as industries are concerned about the risks associated with AI (Deloitte 2019). Research suggests that there will be an unprecedented change to the way work is conducted in the next decades (WEF 2018; ManpowerGroup 2019; Susskind 2020). While some industries will experience boosted productivity, others will not because they may fail to reap advantages or experience demise due to more powerful AI-armed competitors (ACS 2020). For example, the mining and energy extraction industry sectors have made Australia one of the richest countries in the world (EY 2019; Australian Mining 2019). Currently, these industries are taking advantage of advances in robotics, automation, AI and machine learning to solve remote mine sites issues, the hazardous nature of the work, and the high costs of labour and transport (Australian Mining 2019). Different technologies are being used across the mining value chain (exploration, mining operations, processing, transport, trading, and end-to-end). Some of them are AI, machine learning, 3D simulation and modelling, autonomous assets and drilling, digital twin, truckless system, data analytics and visualization, electrification, hyper-spectral core imaging, centre of excellence, integrated operating centre, blockchain, and smart contracts (EY 2019).

As a result, these organizations have improved efficiency and productivity, resulting in greater profitability. However, recent research from approximately a hundred respondents including different industries, shows a mismatch between perceived levels of the strategic importance of AI to the success of business and the urgency and readiness due to a lack of focussed AI strategies (Deloitte 2019). In the mining industry, the total estimated investment in technology required is between $9.4 to $35.2 billion, and the estimated investment in people is between $5.0 to $12.8 billion (EY 2019). The intrinsic risk is a lack of investment in human resource development (Nankervis et al. 2019). The new technology and new ways of working leads to an underlying risk that needs to be managed (EY 2019). Research predicts that by 2034 while automation will displace 2.7 million Australian workers (equivalent to 21 per cent of the workforce), technology is destined to induce 4.5 new million new positions for Australian workers representing a 15 per cent capacity increase within Australian businesses (ACS 2020). Therefore, re-skilling the workforce is crucial to prevent long-term structural unemployment and rising inequality as Nankervis et al. (2019) argued.

To increase the knowledge concerning the challenges of Australian organizations in relation to AI and bearing in mind the huge impact of AI in the Australian workforce, this chapter now focuses on the perception of human resource (HR) departments of Australian organizations on AI. The effective application of AI to HR also presents different challenges that affect the overall aspects of organizations (Tambe et al. 2019). Some of these challenges include 'the fact that data science analyses – when applied to decisions about people – can create serious conflicts with what society typically sees as important for making consequential decisions about individuals' (Tambe et al. 2019, 16). Organizations are comprised of people, and where conflict increases in workplaces through insecurity as a result of the perceived impact of AI, significant problems are likely to arise (Tanmbe et al. 2019; Nankervis et al. 2019). We concede that this is a major issue. This chapter makes a modest contribution to respond to what Nankervis et al. (2019) also declared as a problem due to the sparsity of academic research on perceptions and readiness of HR leaders to tackle the impending disruption AI will induce for staff and industry, particularly in the Australia context.

To understand perceptions of HR departments on AI in the Australian industries context, we build on data collected in 2018 through a series of focus groups performed in four states around Australia. The next sections highlight the methodology used in this study, followed by findings and conclusion.

## Methodology

To gain an in-depth understanding of social issues in relation to how the HR units perceive the Australian readiness on AI, this study used a qualitative methodology approach through focus groups (O.Nyumba et al. 2018). The focus group discussion technique relates to a group of individuals who discuss a complicated topic, to elicit information from their personal experiences, beliefs, perceptions and attitudes of the participants. This was achieved with the interaction of a moderator or facilitator (Hayward et al. 2004). Hence, the researcher (as facilitator) takes a peripheral, rather than a centre-stage position during focus group deliberations (Bloor et al. 2001).

This study builds on data collected in 2018 from RMIT University in collaboration with the Australian Human Resources Institute (AHRI). The number of participants per focus group averaged five (nineteen in total), and focus group discussion sessions were conducted in Melbourne, Perth, Adelaide, Sydney and Newcastle with each lasting approximately 60 minutes. To understand perceptions of AI and to apply the principle of theoretical saturation (Krueger 1994), the composition of the group was not only HR professionals but also middle- and high-level executives from different industries including finance services sector, law, education, manufacturing, travel, health and welfare, communication and transport and utilities/energy industries. The age of participants was spread evenly from approximately 25 to 50 years of age. The participant recruitment process was organized by AHRI through an advertisement with AHRI's members, and focus groups were held in AHRI's offices. Questions used during discussions (see appendix) were around AI and HR, and AI and policy interventions, and the data was analysed through the aid of NVivo10 software.

## Findings

We have organized our findings into eight themes: Perception on AI; transition to AI; strategy involving AI (strategy-finance and strategy-Ethics); government concerning to AI; industry type (AI effects on industry type); HR/HR professionals (HR and ethics, HR and HR AI systems, work balance, HR strategy, HR-skill shortages); fear; and frustration.

## *Perception on AI*

In general, the perception of participants about the adoption of AI and the transformation process is that Australia is not ready. As stated by a participant, 'We're so far behind, you know.' Findings also indicate that organizations (1) need clear information about the applicability of AI, (2) need more collaboration than competitiveness, and (3) face a lack of government support. In addition, when SMEs are struggling to reach local and global competitiveness due to the lack of AI solutions, multinational enterprises (MNEs) from Australia or with headquarters in Australia are driving their businesses further using the latest technologies, products, software and tools to enhance productivity.

## *Transition to AI*

As a tool to accelerate the transition, participants argued that AI plays an important role in enabling a systemic shift within the organization. The use of models and systems accelerates work activities leading to improved productivity. Because transition into AI promotes change, the transition was also associated with how change management is conducted and managed (or mismanaged) during the process. Some concepts related to change management included not only making task management more efficient to accelerate processes, identifying and mitigating risks easily, and changing the mindset of as many people in the organization as strategies will allow. The transition process is moving from transactional to transformational, where transparency, honesty and a holistic approach are crucial to achieve effectives in the adoption of AI. For example, a respondent said, 'I think transition is a huge issue in change management in terms of how people and/or organizations […] where change is just absolutely stratospheric and so rapid.'

## *Strategy Involving AI*

The strategy involved two sub-themes: strategy-finance and strategy-ethics. Findings advise that strategy may need to include financial planning. Participants argued that small and medium enterprises (SMEs) might need financial assistance to be able to get at the edge of technological advances, and to be able to compete at local and international level. One respondent said, 'Then when they [candidates] get there [to start working in a SME], they don't want to feel like they've been deskilled because they don't have the tools they've got used to in other sectors.'

In addition, strategies may need to involve different stakeholders, including employees and shareholders. A priority is for strategies to be aligned to employment relations including unions. A subsequent strategy may need to include results from analysis on potential effects of AI on societies where organizations operate. In general, respondents suggested that establishing strategic planning to respond to the transition process is a key step in succeeding during the organizational transformation. Strategic planning is also associated in the way technology affects strategic planning itself, including decision-making systems. A respondent highlighted that 'when you don't have strategic planning and thinking right at the forefront then you've got implications down the pathway'.

### Government in Relation to AI

In general, participants were not aware if the government had developed any AI initiatives. What the findings show is the view that the Australian government (1) needs to invest by providing financial support in particular for SMEs, (2) commitment and strategies to assist Australian organizations, (3) and clear policies. 'I think there are no existing policies at the moment, not that I'm aware of.'

### Industry Type (Effects of AI on Industry Type)

The type of industry determines different implications and challenges in relation to the applicability or adoption of AI. For example, in some industries (such as oil and gas), the number of staff is increasing due to the adoption of new technologies; other industries (such as NGOs) struggle to be up to date with new technologies. Some respondents said that 'the power that big organizations have is that they can have a technology roadmap'; 'from the consulting perspective we're [in] very early days so we haven't had too much opportunity'.

### HR/HR Professionals

The area of HR was discussed in different contexts: HR and ethics, HR and HR AI systems, work balance, HR and strategy, and HR and skill shortages. While responses show the importance of HR professionals to take the lead on the adoption of AI and the need for them to have the right skills to manage AI team capabilities, they also acknowledge that the perception of HR departments in Australia is still viewed as the company 'police'. Findings also suggested that HR needs to remain contemporary, such as merging AI into HR, and while it offers HR the potential for effective organizational processes, careful decision-making is still required by HR professionals to research and ensure the correct AI products are implemented with ethical consideration uppermost in the strategic thinking. Hence, HR needs to be integrated into the organizational strategies and to have a seat at the executive board level. HR also needs to be linked with ethics to manage people during the change, involving different stakeholders, and be linked strongly to employment relations within the organization to achieve an effective organizational transformation.

The focus group findings also showed the need for more technically skilled people to adopt AI and automation. Respondents suggested the need to develop organizational reskilling strategies, by creating organizational learning centres, partnering with universities or technological institutes (such as TAFE), and upgrading teaching curriculum to deliver graduates who meet the requirements needs of industries. A participant said, 'Who is going to be the conscious keeper for an organisation and I think HR has a sort of role in that sort of space.' Another participant said, 'We continue to have abysmal failures in apprenticeships; we have a huge attrition of first year university, because we're not getting that part of the puzzle right.'

### Fear

The acquisition and adoption of AI also produced a sense of fear. Findings show that when organizations are concerned about 'if technology fails' or 'when things go wrong', then people in the organization would 'blame AI systems'. Responses also suggested potential generational issues, for example, when millennials are at the edge of technological knowledge, perhaps generations X and Y may need to retire earlier; or the difficulty of managing teams with tech knowledge when managers lack that knowledge. Other organizations are not moving towards the AI transformational era until they see positive results from other firms: 'They won't go ahead, and they won't move forward until they've seen somebody else.' Other factors are mentioned in different themes, such as the lack of finance, ethical compliances and redundancies.

### Frustration

Some participants expressed frustration at not being able to be compete on a global scale; to see how Australian organizations are very slow in adapting to new technological changes; to understand how to integrate old and new systems or how to integrate the IT and HR departments; and to choose the right AI solutions and providers: 'How much time it's going to take before people switch on, I think we're very slow in adapting to technology and as a result of that I think it creates the pain of people within the organization.'

## Conclusion

Findings from data collected in 2018 reveal that Australia has been tardy in turning to address the AI challenges. Australia needs to change the perception of HR and reinvent HR units to drive effective organizational transformation. This confirms results from Deloitte (2019) on the mismatch between perceived levels of the strategic importance of AI to achieve business success and the urgency and readiness due to the lack of proper AI strategies in Australia. Despite this, recent internal and external factors are contributing to accelerating the transformation era. One of the most important factors is the current COVID-19 crisis, which has fast-tracked the implementation of new technologies and fast learning of processes among different generations of employees within organizations. Other factors relate to the presence of several offshore MNEs offering AI solutions in Australia and new local SMEs offering innovative AI products or services. These companies are enhancing organizational confidence and accelerating adoption of solutions in AI, automation, big data and analytics, blockchain, cloud, cybersecurity, immersive simulation, the Internet of Things and systems integration (Australian Trade Commission 2017).

## References

ACS. 2020. Technology impacts on the Australian workforce, accessed 10 April 2020, https://www.acs.org.au/insightsandpublications/reports-publications/technology-impacts-on-the-australian-workforce.html.

Acemoglu, D., and Robinson, J. A. (2012). *Why Nations Fail: The Origins of Power, Prosperity, and Poverty*. London: Profile Books.

Australian Institute for Machine Learning (AIML). 2019. Our research. Adelaide University. Accessed 14 April 2020, https://www.adelaide.edu.au/aiml/our-research.

Australian Mining. 2019. How mining companies are using AI, machine learning and robots. Accessed 10 May 2020, https://www.australianmining.com.au/features/how-mining-companies-are-using-ai-machine-learning-and-robots/.

Australian Trade Commission, (2017). Australian disruptive technologies. Accessed 25 May 2019, https://www.austrade.gov.au/ArticleDocuments/1358/Australian_Disruptive_Technologies-Industry-Capability-Report.pdf.aspx.

Bloor, M., Frankland, J., Thomas, M., and Robson, K. 2001. *Focus Groups in Social Research*. Thousand Oaks, CA: Sage Publications.

Deloitte Access Economics (DAE). 2018. ACS Australia's digital pulse driving Australia's international ICT competitiveness and digital growth 2018. Accessed 20 April 2020, https://www.acs.org.au/content/dam/acs/acs-publications/aadp2018.pdf.

Deloitte, 2019. Future in the balance? How countries are pursuing an AI advantage. Accessed 27 April 2020, http://images.content.deloitte.com.au/Web/DELOITTEAUSTRALIA/%7Bee93f452-8e39-4d2d-80b3-40fee296bea3%7D_20190502-eme-inbound-how-countries-are-pursuing-an-ai-advantage-report.pdf?utm_source=eloqua&utm_medium=lp&utm_campaign=20190502-eme-how-countries-pursuing-ai&utm_content=cta.

Department of Defence Science and Technology (DDST). 2020. Department of Defence Science and Technology. Australian Government Canberra. Accessed 12 May 2020, https://www.dst.defence.gov.au/.

Department of Industry, Science, Energy and Resources (DISER), Australian Government. 2020. Artificial intelligence. Accessed 12 May 2020. https://www.industry.gov.au/strategies-for-the-future/artificial-intelligence

Elliott, A. 2019a. A $23 trillion opportunity: Why Australia must embrace the AI revolution. The Conversation. Accessed 9 May 2020, https://www.smartcompany.com.au/startupsmart/analysis/australia-ai-revolution/.

———. 2019b. How Australia can make AI work for our economy, and for our people. The Conversation. Accessed 9 May 2020, https://theconversation.com/how-australia-can-make-ai-work-for-our-economy-and-for-our-people-113744.

Ernst and Young (EY). 2019. Future of work: The economic implications of technology and digital mining. A report to the Minerals Council of Australia. Accessed 30 April 2020, https://minerals.org.au/sites/default/files/190214%20The%20Future%20of%20Work%20The%20economic%20implications%20of%20technology%20and%20digital%20mining.pdf.

Future of Life Institute, 2020. AI Policy – Australia. Accessed 4 April 2020, https://futureoflife.org/ai-policy-australia/.

Global Economic Forum (GEF). 2017. The global economy will be $16 trillion bigger by 2030 thanks to AI. Accessed 26 April 2020, https://www.weforum.org/agenda/2017/06/the-global-economy-will-be-14-bigger-in-2030-because-of-ai/.

Hayward, C., Simpson, L., and Wood, L. 2004. Still left out in the cold: Problematising participatory research and development. *Sociologia Ruralis*, 44(1): 95–108.

Krueger, R. A. 1994. *Focus Groups: A Practical Guide for Applied Research*. Thousand Oaks, CA: Sage Publications.

ManpowerGroup. 2019. Humans wanted: Robots need you. ManpowerGroup (Global). Accessed 5 February 2020, https://www.manpowergroup.com/wps/wcm/connect/84b36237-eb5e-460b-bd52-35c28ab187a9/MPG_WEF_SkillsRevolution_4.0_paper_lo.pdf?MOD=AJPERES&CONVERT_TO=URL&CACHEID=84b36237-eb5e-460b-bd52-35c28ab187a9.

Morgan, D. L. 1988. *Focus Group as Qualitative Research*. Newbury Park, CA: Sage Publications.

Nankervis, A., Connell, J., Cameron, R., Montague, A., and Prikshat, V. 2019. 'Are we there yet?' Australian HR professionals and the Fourth Industrial Revolution. *Asia Pacific Journal of Human Resources*. doi:10.1111/1744-7941.12245.

O. Nyumba, T., Wilson, K., Derrick, C., and Mukherjee, N. 2018. The use of focus group discussion methodology: Insights from two decades of application in conservation. *Methods in Ecology and Evolution*, 9(1), 20–32.

Organisation for Economic Co-operation and Development, Artificial Intelligence (OECD.AI). 2020. Policy initiatives for Australia. Accessed 5 May 2020, https://oecd.ai/dashboards/policy-initiatives?conceptUris=http:%2F%2Fkim.oecd.org%2FTaxonomy%2FGeographicalAreas%23Australia.

PricewaterhouseCoopers (PwC). 2017. Sizing the prize: What's the real value of AI for your business and how can you capitalise? Accessed 8 May 2020, http://preview.thenewsmarket.com/Previews/PWC/DocumentAssets/476830.pdf.

Susskind, D. 2020. *A World without Work: Technology, Automation, and How We Should Respond*. New York: Metropolitan Books..

Syam, N., and Sharma, A. 2018. Waiting for a sales renaissance in the fourth industrial revolution: Machine learning and artificial intelligence in sales research and practice. *Industrial Marketing Management*, 69: 135–46.

Tambe, P., Cappelli, P., and Yakubovich, V. 2019. Artificial intelligence in human resources management: Challenges and a path forward. *California Management Review*, 61(4): 15–42.

World Economic Forum. 2018. The future of jobs report. 2018. Insight Report. Geneva: World Economic Forum. Accessed 14 April 2020, http://www3.weforum.org/docs/WEF_Future_of_Jobs_2018.pdf.

## Appendix

Questions used during the focus groups

1   Can you outline your experience in HRM and the respective industry sectors where you work?

2   As employees are likely to experience multiple forms of changes in work practices, job design, and employment status, what policy government policy interventions do you consider to be essential?

3   What policy intervention are you aware of at government levels?

4   What are the anticipated workforce and specific occupational impacts of artificial, robotic and machine learning technologies on different Australian industry sectors in the next decade?

5   In your company have you or do you plan to make use of artificial intelligence or robotics in operations or the HR function? If so, what steps are you taking to manage this implementation?

6   What observations can you outline in terms of the impact in your industry sector now due to changes artificial intelligence, automation and technology are causing?

7   How prepared are HRM professionals to balance the adverse and positive effects of these technologies on their own workforces and in specific occupations?

8   Are there innovative case studies in different industry sectors which illustrate effective principles and practices for HR professionals to develop in addressing the Fourth Industrial Revolution?

# Chapter 14

# CONCLUSION

## J. Mark Munoz and Alka Maurya

The chapters in this book highlight the fact that AI is alive and well in many corners of the world. It is evident that in diverse shapes and forms, AI is having an impact on businesses, governments, economies and lives of people worldwide.

From the chapters, five key themes are notable with regard to the international practice of AI:

**Common appeal** – it is evident that countries in different parts of the world find AI appealing and are using it to advance operational efficiencies.

**Diversity of application** – while there is common interest in AI worldwide, countries and companies differ with regard to what they view as priorities or essential to their operations.

**Lack of cooperation** – it appears that AI is used and applied in different locations in silos and there is not much cross-country collaboration seen.

**Economic importance** – from the modalities in which AI is applied, it is evident that the practice of AI translates into a significant economic impact.

**Technological reliance** – the success of AI applications in countries is dependent on the technological infrastructure, resources and talent available in the location.

These themes suggest the following:

1. **AI impacts a nation's competitiveness** – countries that invest in AI and have the technological framework to implement and advance AI would gain a competitive edge.

**Table 14.1** Strategic highlights for governments

| | |
|---|---|
| Cross-country collaboration | Governments need to seek out ways to collaborate with other countries to boost their AI competencies. |
| Technological investment | Governments need to commit to invest in infrastructure and skill development to optimize gains from AI. |
| In-country coordination | Governments should explore AI developments already taking place in academia or in the corporate sector and find ways to spread them throughout the country as a means for job creation, economic development and productivity enhancement. |
| Strategic planning | Governments need to plan ahead and create a five- year strategic plan to optimize benefits relating to AI. |
| Innovation-driven policies | Governments need to plan for and implement policies that support and accelerate AI in their countries. |

2. **Cross-country cooperation can bolster AI competencies** – since country infrastructure and resources are uneven, the sharing of resources can lead to mutual benefits.

3. **Advancement in AI in countries impacts corporate performance and lives of the citizenry** – a country with a well-developed AI architecture provides essential support for corporations as well as government organizations, which in turn improves the lives of its citizenry.

In light of the above, the authors suggest the following courses of actions for governments, corporations, and executives and entrepreneurs.

## Governments

Table 14.1 outlines important strategic considerations for governments.

These strategies underscore the fact that gaining advantages in AI does not happen by accident. For governments to optimize the economic benefits relating to AI, careful planning and well-conceived supporting investments are necessary.

## Corporations

Table 14.2 outlines important strategic considerations for corporations.

These strategies suggest that corporations need to think in new ways. They need to aspire to be 'cognitive leaders' in their field. Firms that utilize AI to the fullest will likely gain a competitive advantage over those that don't.

**Table 14.2** Strategic highlights for corporations

| | |
|---|---|
| Cross-country collaboration | Corporations need to seek out ways to collaborate with companies in other countries to boost their AI competencies. |
| Technological investment | Corporations need to invest in infrastructure and skill development to optimize gains from AI. |
| Creative collaborations | Corporations need to explore ways to tap AI breakthroughs in academia and other sectors in order to optimize operational efficiencies, enhance customer interactions, improve products or boost profitability. Internal or intra-company collaboration should also be enhanced in order to effectively use AI within the organization. |
| Strategic planning | Corporations need to plan ahead and create a five-year strategic plan to optimize benefits relating to AI. |
| Innovation-driven policies | Corporations need to plan for and implement policies that support and accelerate AI in their organizations. |

**Table 14.3** Strategic highlights for executives and entrepreneurs

| | |
|---|---|
| Global mindset | Executives and entrepreneurs need to explore AI opportunities not only within their countries but worldwide in order to gain unique business advantages. |
| Technological investment | Executives and entrepreneurs need to invest in technological products as well as in skill development to optimize gains from AI both within an organizational and personal context. |
| Creative collaborations | Executives and entrepreneurs should explore ways to tap AI advancements in academia and in other sectors to further their business agenda. The possibilities are endless with regard to the types of collaborations that can be formed. |
| Personal development plan | Executives and entrepreneurs need to create a personal development plan to stay up to date with the fast-changing trends and developments in the field of AI. Acquisition of AI-related skills can and will be beneficial. |
| Entrepreneurial attitude | Executives and entrepreneurs will be exposed to several business opportunities relating to AI in the coming years. Keeping an open mind as well as an entrepreneurial attitude can lead to the discovery of unique opportunities down the road. |

## Executives and Entrepreneurs

Table 14.3 outlines important strategic considerations for executives and entrepreneurs.

These strategies imply that executives and entrepreneurs will be exposed to a wave of opportunities in the field of AI in the coming years. The ability to strategically scrutinize and act on the best opportunities can lead to financial breakthroughs.

With advancements in the field of AI simultaneously happening around the world, society is living through a new normal. As such, there no longer is a status quo. AI is constantly reshaping governments and businesses, and a new paradigm needs to be in place.

Three new international organizations can help shape the future of AI worldwide.

**AI International Chamber of Commerce** – a global business association solely focused on the advancement of AI in the field of business can be beneficial to businesses worldwide.

**AI International Regulatory Council** – a global organization that sets the rules with regard to AI can mitigate some of the challenges and risks associated with the advancements in AI.

**AI Global Forum** – a global entity comprised of member nations can hold annual forums regarding the challenges and opportunities regarding AI. These forums can be the venue to strengthen country collaborations as well as setting parameters and boundaries in the use of AI.

While the field of AI is growing in leaps and bounds and impacts many organizations in a positive way, risks and challenges do exist. With companies and countries operating in silos, efficiency is not optimized. Furthermore, with the multitude of AI advancements happening worldwide, there is a fairly high risk that a country or company may misuse it or apply it unethically. When this is unchecked there could be dire consequences.

AI is both an opportunity and a threat. Within a global landscape, opportunities and threats are magnified.

AI belongs to the world. As a global community, we need to jointly think about it not only as a strategic tool for economic development but as a way to create global harmony and safeguard humanity.

This book on the international perspectives on AI clearly shows that there is no stopping AI. The future of AI is both exciting and daunting. The steps we take as governments, companies, executives and entrepreneurs will define its future course.

# INDEX

Note: Bold number indicates the figure.

Lightning Source UK Ltd.
Milton Keynes UK
UKHW010843271221
396203UK00002B/66